Wealth 101 for Women Entrepreneurs

Natalie Grignon

Dedication

To my children; being a mother made me want to be a good person for myself, for you and for my community.

To all of you whom I have met,

Whether you are currently part of my life or have been in the past; You helped shaped my life. All that we have loved deeply became part of us.

I am blessed & grateful.

ISBN :   978-1-9994684-6-0

Although the author has made every effort to ensure that the information in this book was correct at press time, the author does not assume and hereby disclaim any liability to any party for any loss, damage, or disruption caused by errors or omissions, whether such errors or omissions result from negligence, accident, or any other cause. The information in this book is meant to supplement, not replace, the advice given by your advisor.

Book design by author.
Illustration by @thanksinsomnia at Fiverr.com
Author Photograph by : Chantale Arsenault

Other books by the same author :

Wealth 101 for teenagers

ISBN: 978-1-9994684-0-8

Richesse 101 pour ados :

ISBN: 978-1-9994684-2-2

Divorce Financial Analysis ; how a CDFA can help with your family law practice.

ISBN: 978-1-9994684-5-3

The list might change by the time this book is published.

en·tre·pre·neur

/ˌäntrəprəˈnər, ˌäntrəprəˈno͞o(ə)r/

- Noun
- A person who organizes and operates a business or businesses, taking on greater than normal financial risks in order to do so.

Woman
en·tre·pre·neur

/ˈwo͞omən/

/ˌäntrəprəˈnər, ˌäntrəprəˈno͞o(ə)r/

- Noun
- *A woman, (who has a lot of stuff on her plate already but wants to better the life of her family),* who organizes and operates a business or businesses, taking on greater than normal financial risks in order to do so.

Contents

Building wealth is not summarized in one paragraph. Besides winning the lottery or doing extremely well with a stock, most individuals who build wealth do it slowly, over time. In this book, you will find things that help you build wealth, and things that hinder it.

<u>Introduction</u>

<u>Knowing your numbers</u>
1) Knowing your numbers
2) Control your expenses.

<u>Your financial information and tools</u>

3) Have the proper advising team
4) Understanding inflation and how it affects your wealth
5) Understanding the magic of compound interest
6) Stocks
7) Mutual funds
8) GIC's
9) Registered Accounts
10) Individual RESP vs Group RESP
11) Your pension

Introduction

I was 21 when I owned my first business.

I have learned a lot from that experience.

I had a coffee shop and was trying to get pregnant at the same time. (I never actually admitted this to my business partner. How can you start a business and try to get pregnant? - that would be anyone's reaction) I admit, not the ideal. But I was 4 years old when I decided that I could have it all. Love, career, kids, and house. Everything.

We can have it all, but you cannot have kids and a blooming career (or business) unless you have a daycare, or a nanny.

This is the struggle of most mothers I meet. We want to have children, and we are truly in love with being a mother. We also want a career, to feel fulfilled. Feeling needed for our abilities other than being able to change a diaper or winning an argument with a 2-year-old.

I was driven but felt awful about my ambitions. When we take time away from our kids, we feel like a bad mom. When we are at home on a Sunday morning watching Teletubbies or Barney (yes, that is how old I am) , we feel inadequate that we did not sneak in at work to finish some things. This struggle is real for a lot of women.

Society has told us that we can have it all. Be a great mother who cooks perfect meals and bakes 5 dozen cookies for the holiday season. Make killer presentations and close deals faster than your male colleagues....

I wanted it all. But something had to give. For me, for many years, it was the laundry and shoes in the entrance. (how come it looks like we are 20 people living in the freaking house....) . The husband getting mad every time he helped clean the washroom or the dishes. The comment: 'I help you with the kids' was often said. Weird comment for a father to say, I thought. They are your kids as well. You are simply taking care of them (not helping me take care of them. Because I am a mother, I am supposed to take care 100% of their needs?) A little glimpse into a marriage that would not last. But in that moment, I never responded to that stupid comment. Too much stuff to do, do not have time to start a fight....

On top of it all, we, women, judge each other. It is so easy to judge.

The stay-at-home mom, or the single mom who is on welfare and trying to get her life together after an abusive relationship.

I come from one of those homes, a rough childhood where school was not an escape. My days filled with bullies and fear. It is hurtful being judged for being poor or coming from a broken home. I now live my life as judgement-free as possible.

My past created who I am, and I am grateful. My experience owning the coffee shop, and my career as an Investment Advisor, taught me so much about building wealth and being an entrepreneur.

So this book is for all women trying to better their lives by starting a business. Any business, any size.

Building wealth.

Slow and steady.

You need to know your numbers.

Chapter one
Knowing your
numbers.

We often get asked questions about what stock is the next big thing. Should I invest in this, in that...

I want to invest in something that will make me super-rich, but you know, without the risk of losing my money. Ask anyone working in the financial services field, we get this often.
The truth is, to build real wealth; you need discipline, time and a lot of common sense.

No matter if you have a lot of money already, or you are just starting out, I will always start my relationship with you talking about the basis, knowing your numbers.
How can you make a financial plan and grow your net worth, if you don't know where you are right now?

I will ask your personal information, like your salary, your debts. This might feel like such an invasion of privacy, but for us, who has been doing this for a long time, they are just numbers. You might have $2,000 of debt, or $2million. Just numbers to plug into a financial-planning software. No judgement. This is math, logic, compounding-interest.

Any advisor will ask you these questions, not only because it is needed, but it is also a requirement from our regulatory bodies. We are governed by the 'know-your-client' rule. But before asking you these questions, we have chatted, we have met a couple of times. If we are sitting in this meeting, it is because you want to work with me.

These are the numbers you should know:
- How much money you make, from all sources.
- Monthly budget
- List of assets (type of asset, value, where it is held)
- List of debts (amount, type of debt)
- Information on your Group Plan at work
- Information on your individual insurance products
- How much RRSP/TFSA room you have (this is found on the CRA web site.)
- Did you open a FHSA in 2023? (or planning to open one?
- Did you receive an inheritance, or think you will receive one?

How much money you make, from all sources.

This might sound obvious, and a silly to question to ask. Do you really know how much money you make per month?

For some, it is easy, just look at the last paychecks.

For some, who are entrepreneurs, their income varies, per month and per year. Let's look at the last 3 years, for example. Did your income dramatically increase or decrease? Should we take the average of the last 6 months?

Do you have multiple sources of income?
Do you have a parent who sends you money once in a while?
I am not even going to ask if you have a sugar-daddy (or sugar-mommy)

You might not even take into consideration some sources of income in your calculations. For example, you have a book out, and make maybe $3000 per year with it, but since it is a small amount, you do not calculate it.

What about the tax credits and or benefits? Do you get the Canada Child Benefit, GST credit, Disability tax credit, or provincial credits ?
(Since I am in Canada, I mention these credits. Make sure you know about all of the tax credits or benefits in your area)

Why it is important to list everything?

Once you make your budget, and write sown all the yearly expenses, you might have a deficit on paper which is not the reality.

I once told a client:
"Looks like you are short of about $500 per month."

Her answer: " no, my ex-boyfriend, who is not the biological father of the children, but who was in our lives for 8 years , gives me about $300 - $600 per month. He knows I use the amount on the kids". (This is not the real information, for the sake of not revealing the true story of the person I was talking to).   Since the money is not a guarantee, and never the same, she did not include it in her budget. It is not her reality though. AND if she stops receiving an amount from him, she was clearly under every month.

For most people, not everything is calculated to the dollar. BUT you should do the exercise at least once per year.

Monthly budget

This might be overwhelming for someone starting out, especially if you are not organised. Also overwhelming for someone who has been in a long-term relationship and was not the one in control of the finances. It is never too late. Remember that men die an average of eight years before women, so let's not wait until the husband passes away before we look at numbers. (I often get the 'pfffft, it is my husband who takes care of it') If you are talking about an oil change, that is great, but finance? Not so much. Let's change that.

I bet the term *monthly budget* struck a chord for some of you.

The following is the rule I have been following. It is a wake-up call. It confirms that we NEED to keep our expenses much lower than we think.

The rule is the 50-30-20 rule. If you follow this, especially at a younger age, financial success will be much easier to achieve.

The 50-30-20 rule:

This budgeting rule was coined by Elizabeth Warren, a U.S Senator.

It represents:

50% of your net income for NEEDS.   I always calculate net income; it does not make sense to try to use gross. (and it would come to the same thing, as this is a ratio that equals 100%)

Needs: 50%

Mortgage or rent.

Hydro

Groceries

Transportation (car payment or bus pass)

Gas

Insurance.

Wants: 30%

30% seems like a lot for wants, as we are told to reduce those as much as possible. In reality a lot of our expenses fall under this: shopping, WIFI, CELL, cable, entertainment, restaurants, birthdays, holiday expenses, daycare, hobbies, travel.

For some, they add the gas in this section, they say they mostly spend on gas for non-job-related outings like grocery shopping, etc

You can put some expenses here, like hydro, if you prefer. Either way, both of these categories together make up 80%.

Savings and debt: 20%

I know that the rule of thumb used to be 10% savings. But let's face it. If you are in your late forties and do not have any savings, your savings should even be at 25% or more.

At twenty percent of savings, it keeps you alert of your spending.

Let's look at some numbers:

Here is a pretty realistic example :

Total monthly income :		3 200,00 $
50 % needs		
Rent	1 000,00 $	
hydro	120,00 $	
car payment	- $	
bus pass	110,00 $	
home insurance	70,00 $	
car insurance	50,00 $	
groceries	400,00 $	
Total needs :	1 750,00 $	
Percentage of total needs		55%
30% wants		
Wifi, cable, cell	300,00 $	
restaurants and entertainment, gas	200,00 $	
Travel (saving for travel)	200,00 $	
other insurance	300,00 $	
Medical	100,00 $	
total wants	1 100,00 $	
Percentage of total wants		34%
Savings		
Save the rest	350,00 $	
Percentage of total savings		11%

Make a list here of your NEEDS:

Rent or mortgage:

Taxes (if not included in the mortgage payment):

Hydro

Home and car insurance

Car payment

Gas

Groceries

<u>Make a list here of your WANTS:</u>

CELL

Cable

WIFI

Shopping

Entertainment

Daycare or teenagers' social lives

Hobbies

Travel

Restaurants and coffee

Birthdays and holidays

Car repairs

Home repairs

Medical and dental

Accounting or other professional fees

Yearly things like Costco membership, and snow removal

<u>Make a list here of your SAVINGS and debt plans:</u>

- In the ideal world, are you putting money in :
- Paying down debt
- Putting money for an emergency fund
- RESP (registered educational savings plan)
- FHSA (first home savings account)
- RRSP (registered retirement savings plan)
- TFSA (Tax-free savings account)
- Nom-registered account (this is a fully taxable account)
- Crypto (not necessarily a recommendation)

For a lot of people, once we go over the budget and it reveals the real numbers, they realise they spend too much. I wish I could just tell you to stop spending. Stop the need to have a house, or a fancier house, to look rich and successful. Just stop.

List of assets.

This is a nice list to go over every year, and it is needed to calculate your net worth. Ideally, your net worth should go up every year.

Your net worth is :

Assets
Minus
Liabilities

Make a list of your assets [1]:
- its market value[2].
- its ACB (adjusted cost base)[3]
- where it is held.

[1]: An asset is something that has value, that we can sell. From a toaster, a computer, a car, a house, stocks, investments, Air Miles, boats, real estate, cash value from a life insurance policy. We don't necessarily write down all the things we own (for example: a toaster, a coffee machine, etc.). But if separating, you might have to write down everything.

[2]: Market value is what someone is willing to pay. For real estate, you will ask your agent. For the market value of your investments, you will look at your monthly account statement. For things like a boat and a car, there is a 'black book', if I am not mistaken.

[3]: ACB: Adjusted Cost base, simply put, is the price you paid for it, but not 100% exact. The price you paid plus commission (like in a stock) Or the price you paid, plus legal fees, notary fees and commissions (like an investment property). For investments inside a TFSA, for example, we don't pay too much attention to the ACB once we sell, because there is no gain nor loss in a TFSA. However, in a non-registered account, trading always takes into consideration the ACB. (I once had a client whose ACB was $10K, and the market value was $100K, that is a $90K gain to declare, if she had sold) . There are more things to discover about the ACB's, which can be found on the Revenu Canada website.

Example of a list of assets:

Type of asset	Owner	Market value	ACB	Where it is held
House	both	500 000,00 $		
Cottage	me	300 000,00 $	50 000,00 $	
Non-registered account	me	50 000,00 $	30 000,00 $	Sunlife
RRSP	me	50 000,00 $		CIBC Wood Gundy
TFSA	me	50 000,00 $		RBC

Anything that is taxable at sale, like real estate investments or investments in a non-registered account, you have to keep track of the ACB.

For registered accounts like the TFSA, your account statement will show your ACB, which is nice to know. But you do not consider the ACB when calculating your net worth because it is a tax-free account.

Sone people add much more in their list of assets.
You can even make a distinction between liquid assets, like your investments, or not as liquid like art.

You can add you car, (and add the total payment left on your debt-side).

In the case of a separation, you will also add:

- Furniture and appliances
- Kitchen supplies, including the china
- Kitchen small appliances, including the coffee machines, the panini press, and your favorite blender.
- Baking supplies and appliances
- Alcohol cabinet, including the crystal ice buckets and the Bartesian cocktail machine
- Computers, cameras , video streaming equipement
- Video game consoles and gaming chairs
- Music stereo , and home theatre sets
- Art, stamp, hockey card, figurine collections
- Air Miles, or any other points you have accumulated.
- Time shares, vacation ownership, vacation clubs
- Cash surrender value of Life Insurance Policies
- Tools
- Sports, fish, hunting ad camping equipment
- Party supplies, including the dry-ice smoke machine.
- Crafting supplies, supplies cabinet, Cricket Machine.
- Books
- Gym equipment
- Expensive bags, like Chanel and Louis Vuitton
- Jewelry

As you can see, making the list of assets will be different depending on the reason. If it is for financing purposes, your banker will not care about all of that. If it is because you are heading towards separation, it is important to keep a list. Keep note that the market value of most household items will be the "garage-sale' price. So your couch that you paid $2000, will now have a market value of $400, if that.

In the chart above, the column "Where it is held" is useful for :
- If you have many real estate properties, you write the address.
- If you have a Group RRSP, you want to remember where it is.
- In case of your incapacity, or death, your liquidator should know where your stuff is.
- I never recommend having accounts in many institutions, but it is the sad reality. People chase short-term promotions " Open an account here and you will get 5% for 6 months. If you are this type of person, you must create yourself an Excel sheet.
- For couples, where one person controls the finances, this allows the other spouse to have the basic information.

List of debts

This, and making a budget, is the hard part for most people.
(I can tell you that building wealth is ALL about the investments, but it is not the truth.)

A lot of people do not tell us the truth when we ask them about their debt load. There is absolutely no reason to lie to us. We make a financial/ retirement/ estate plan based on the numbers you give us. If the information is wrong, the plan is wrong.

Once, a client called me and asked me to keep the information form her husband. She had a secret credit card with a balance of $5000. There are things you can keep secret for a little bit. But what if both of you want to refinance your home, to purchase another real estate property? The truth will come out if you are hiding debts from your spouse.

Once you are ready to write your list of debts, you will need the statement, because you need this information:
- Balance of credit used.
- Total credit limit
- Rate of interest on purchases
- Rate of interest on cash advance (which you should not do)
- Monthly minimum payment
- If a line of credit, is it a mortgage line of credit, or a persone one?
- F the debt is co-owned.

This is what your Excel sheet could look like :

Type of credit	Account or card number	which bank or firm	Lien on a property ?	interest rate on purchase	interest rate on cash advance	credit used or balance	Credit total	minimum monthly payment
Visa	5258 *** ***	TD		12%	20%	500,00 $	10 000,00 $	10,00
Line of credit	525 ***	TD	yes, house	8%	8%	2 000,00 $	200 000,00 $	40,00
Mortgage	612345	TD	yes, house	5%		200 000,00 $		876,00
Line of credit	4321	TD	no	12%		5 000,00 $	50 000,00 $	200,00
Car loan	9321654	GM/ National Bank	yes, car	9%			35 000,00 $	500,00

By putting all of this information, including the interest rate of your credit cars, it will allow you to come up with a plan.

For example, do you have one card with a higher interest rate?
If so:

- You could contact the financial institution and try to negotiate a lower rate. (Sometimes negotiating a lower rate means changing cards and eliminating the travel points, or other perks. But you must ask yourself if those perks are worth it.
- If a credit account or card has a much lower interest, and plenty of room, you could transfer to it a smaller account with a higher interest rate.
- But, be always mindful that your credit score is affected if your credit cards are more than 40- 50% used. It is better to have 2 cards with a smaller amount, than one card almost full.

Calculating Net Worth

So calculating your net worth is easy if you have listed all of your assets and credit used (liabilities). For liabilities, do not put the monthly or minimum payment, it is the full amount that is left.

Net worth = Assets - liabilities

Type of asset	Market value	ACB	Where it is held
House	500 000,00 $		
Cottage	300 000,00 $	50 000,00 $	
Non-registered account	50 000,00 $	30 000,00 $	Sunlife
RRSP	50 000,00 $		RBC
TFSA	50 000,00 $		RBC
Car	15 000,00 $		
total assets	965 000,00 $		

Liabilities	total owing		
Mortgage house	220 000,00 $		RBC
Cottage mortgage	50 000,00 $		RBC
Car	8 000,00 $		
Visa	2 000,00 $		TD
Ortho	6 000,00 $		
Line of credit	12 000,00 $		TD
total liabilities	298 000,00 $		

Net worth	667 000,00 $		

Calculating net worth is straight forward, but I often have similar questions from clients.

- The house is owned jointly with my spouse, do I enter the full market value, or half?
    - You should enter half, and half the mortgage in the liabilities section.
- Follow-up question: Yes, but if he passes away, the house will belong to me 100%.
    - No, not necessarily. Married? Common-Law? Are there any Wills done? This needs a whole different discussion. (Seen later in this book)

- For our rental properties, do we simply calculate market value minus liability? Because if we sell right now, the number does not represent what we will have in our pocket.
    - To calculate net worth, yes, it is market value minus liability. In the case of a separation, for example, you have to take into consideration a few more things, like commission to the agent, mortgage penalty, Capital Recapture, and gains/loss.
- I have crypto that has lost a lot of value since I invested. I am pretty sure it will go back up. Do I have to put the value of today, or can I put last month's value?
    - You put the market value that reflects the truth. Even if you think the crypto will go back up, it might not. For some assets, like Life Insurance products, you might receive an annual statement only, therefore, you put the latest number you received.

Information on your Group Plan at work

This is a book about women entrepreneurs, why bring up Group Plans?
It is a myth that entrepreneurs do not have access to group plans.
A lot of entrepreneurs that I know have a job with benefits, have a
spouse with benefits, or purchased a private plan.

When someone asked me if they should get life insurance, or Critical
Illness or Disability, my first answer will always be **"depends".**

Depends, because:

- I am not an advisor who will push an insurance policy to make a
  commission. I have never done that, and never will. And it
  shows when this happened, because the client has a bung of
  products not suitable for them.
- I will ask them if the have the basics: a Will, a Mandate,
  individual policies, joint policies?
- Do you have a group plan with an insurance coverage? of so, did
  you purchase optional coverage?
- Do you have coverage on credit products? (you can buy
  "insurance" on bank products like mortgages and credit cards)

Group Plans:

Important points to note:

- There is not a company that has "better" plans for group plans. (disputable, but not my point) For example, Sunlife. A Sunlife rep will meet with the HR of your company. Together they will come up with a plan that they think the employees will be happy with, and that the employer can pay. If you have a friend whose plan is better than yours, it is not because the insurance company is better than the other, it is the plan that was chosen that is better. The employer must be able, or willing, to pay for the better plans.
- There is a general plan that is for everyone, and there might be choices that needs to be done. You might have to make a choice on dental and medical options. And if you want Extra coverage. Those choices seem to be hard for people to make. If you chose the basic dental plan, but then need something that is not covered, will you have the cash to pay for it? (example Crowns or root canals?)
- Insurance, Critical Illness and Disability products in group plans are not guaranteed products. Meaning, if you get sick, you might not get paid. If you get a disability, they might reject your claim. Those products look at your medical file AFTER you submit a claim. Versus when you buy an individual coverage, where they check your medical file BEFORE deciding to cover you or not. (more information on insurance later in this book)
- Do not cancel any extra coverage before talking to your advisor.
- Think twice before taking any of those options, including extra life insurance. Those coverages might be much more expensive than if you had an individual plan.

- Your spouse might be covered for dental or medical expenses, but they are probably NOT covered if they get sick, like cancer. So this means, if your spouse gets sick, you cannot take 6 months off to take care of them. Some group plans have a 'compassionate clause', which allows you to take time off if your spouse, or one of your kids, gets sick. But a lot of people do not have this clause. Thus, the need to each person to have individual, real, coverage.

If we discuss your finances, I will ask you if you have a group plan, and these would be my questions:
- What your coverage is, for life insurance, Disability and Critical Illness
- For life insurance, do you have one time your salary? and did you buy additional? (not a recommendation, just a question)
- For Disability, do you have short-term? Long-term? what are the percentages? Example: 100% or your salary? 50 %?
- What is the coverage period? Example, do you have a maximum of 2 years on disability, or up to age 65?
- For critical illness, what are the details? Do you get a lump sum?
- Are they a taxable benefit?
- Do you have the spousal compassionate care?
- What are the other options you took?
- What is your monthly premium?
- Does your medical and dental coverage cover you for all of your needs? Or do you have to pay out of pocket for glasses and orthodontist?

- If you took the 'best option', would it cover all your needs? Did you compare the higher premium on the best plan, and if it is worth it?
  - For example, paying $50 more a month, but you only go to the dentist once a year, which costs $150.
  - Or paying $50 more a month to be able to go see a masseuse, but you only go three times a year because you do not take the time?
- Ok, I might not ask you all these questions, because you probably do not know. I will ask you for a copy of your booklet though. And I will ask you these questions especially if you want to review your coverage.

Make a list here of your Group Plan questions.

Steps to take now:

1. If you have a Group Plan.

- Download your plan information.
- Look over it and take note of your coverage.
    - Life insurance, what amount?
    - Do you have short-term disability?
    - If so, is it 100% of your salary for 3 months?
    - Do you have long-term?
    - If so :
        - What is the total period of coverage? 2 years, up to age 65? This would mean, if you were to have a disability that is long-term, would they still cover you for only 2 years?
        - What is the percentage? 67% ?
        - What is the monthly maximum? This is important, because the monthly maximum could be MUCH lower than your salary. For people making $65K or more per year should pay attention to this.
        - Does it cover your ''own profession", or does it cover " any' occupation. Meaning, if you're a surgeon, but lose the mobility of your hands, your 'own profession' coverage would pay you. 'Any profession' would mean that the insurance company would not pay, because you would be able to teach.

- o What exactly is your dental coverage?
- o What exactly is your medical coverage?
- Do NOT cancel any extra coverages before talking with your advisor.

2. If you do NOT have a group plan:

- Once you reviewed your budget, decide how much money you can put into monthly premiums for insurance coverages. (life, CI , DI or even accident) . Accident covers you for stupid accidents like falling on ice and breaking a hip, but it does not cover you in case of cancer or depression.
- Make an appointment with your advisor or reach out to an advisor you trust to ask questions.
- Do not let yourself feel rushed into buying a protection, make sure you understand what you are buying, and that the monthly premium is doable.

Information on your other insurance products.

What I am talking about here are the 'insurance' products on credit cards, mortgages, car loans, personal loans and lines of credit.

We have all been asked if we wanted to add insurance protection on our credit card, or other credit products, for "as little as x$ on every $1000 of debt." Sounds like a small amount, but it can add up. (thus, part of knowing your numbers)

Here are the details of those products (life, critical illness, and/or disability)

- You pay what seems like a small amount of money per thousand you have in credit.
- The bank, or creditor, gets paid if something happens to you.
- For example, your mortgage monthly payment would be paid if you were disabled.
- Or your mortgage would be paid completely if you were to pass away.
- These are never guaranteed products, meaning, you could have a disability, but your claim might be refused. (There are plenty of rumors that there are claim-agents who get bonuses when they reject the greatest number of claims.)
- The reason why they are not guaranteed? The products are added to your account within seconds, and without medical questions. Everyone has the same 'coverage' no matter their health or history.

- The creditor gets paid, but nothing is given to your beneficiaries.
- Often those products are more expensive than if you had individual coverage. (depends on your age and health situation)

What to do if you think you have those coverages?

First, take out your account statements, and any credit contract.

Check for any amount that seems to be added to the monthly payment.
- Car loan contract.
- Credit card
- Personal line of credit
- Mortgage line of credit
- Mortgage

Second, make a list: (or contact the financial institution to get more information)

- What type of protection is it? Is it life insurance, critical illness or disability?
  - If it is life insurance, it is easy to understand. The company gets paid the full amount that you owe.
  - If it is a critical illness insurance, or disability, normally your monthly payment is paid for you. (if your claim is accepted) . YOU do not get any money, it is your creditor that gets paid.
- How much is it per month?

Third: do NOT cancel anything. The ideal would be to eliminate all those amounts that are added on your monthly credit payments, and to get a real individual coverage. But you must get the individual coverage first, which could take months, BEFORE you cancel the rest.

Fourth: talk to an advisor you trust. Show them the list of the coverages you pay every month.

Fifth : Once you have individual protections in place, you can contact your bank and cancel the coverages. And the next time someone offers you an added protection, say no. All that extra money could be put in investments instead.

Information on your individual insurance products

There are different types of insurance to consider. Ignoring the importance of insurance is not facing the truth about the real possibility of being sick or dying.

You have a one in three chance of having some sort of disability before the age of 65.
For those with a health issue that lasts more than 90 days, the severity of it lasts about 2.3 years. For example, in the case of cancer.
A disability causes much more financial troubles than if you passed away.
If your budget allows you for very little insurance, talk to an advisor you trust, tell them your budget, and simply start.

This chapter is about knowing your numbers. When making your budget, you will be able to determine how much money you are able to put into savings, investments, and insurance.

Sometimes we have young kids, and everything is so expensive, that we have little money for extra. Should you put a hold on your investments to allow some sort of coverage? Maybe.

By really knowing your numbers, you will be able to put things in place for now and have a plan for the future.

One mistake people do when in a financial difficulty, they cancel their insurance. You should not do that. *You might be able to reduce your coverage*, thus the premium, instead of cancelling.

Types of insurance:

- Term or temporary life insurance
- Permanent life insurance
- Permanent with participations life insurance
- Universal Life life insurance
- Accident insurance
- Critical Illness Insurance
- Disability insurance
- Pet insurance

Some of these insurances can be combined. For example, a permanent insurance of $50,000 with a rider of $200,00 t-10 term insurance. A **rider** is something that is added to a policy, it does not stand alone.

Term or temporary life insurance. This is the most basic type of insurance.

- A temporary insurance for a temporary need. For example, you have young kids, a mortgage, debt, and do not yet see a light at the end of the tunnel.
- This is the most coverage you can get for your buck.
- You have to understand the coverage.
- Normally the term insurance has a level premium for the years you took. For example, a term-10 will have monthly premiums that are the same for the first 10 years. Then, it does NOT terminate, the cost of the monthly premiums go up after.
- Most good policies will offer you a conversion.
    - This means, you can convert into a permanent insurance during a set period of time
    - The conversion is without medical proof. Which is important because your health might have changed.
    - Sometimes you are allowed to convert only a part of it into a permanent and keep also a temporary.
    - Every contract is different, you have to read it.

Permanent life insurance. This is a life insurance that your will keep until you die.

- Ideally, people should buy a basic one when they are young.
- The longer you wait, it becomes harder to afford.
- We often suggest a term policy to people who have a very limited budget. But it is up to you to make the necessary budget arrangements to be able to afford it. I know way too many people who go for the luxurious renting place, or the biggest house possible, but do not have a single insurance product.
- This policy is easy to understand. You pay the same monthly premium until you pass away. The payment never goes up, the death benefit never goes up.
- Pay 20. This policy means that you pay for 20 years but are covered until death. It is a way to pay your policy faster.

Permanent with participations life insurance.

- This policy is the same as above, except it has a savings component in it.
- The savings component leads to a cash value over time.
- You can borrow against the cash value.
- You can cancel your life insurance and get the cash value for it.
- However, don't get too excited, cash value builds slowly.
- Whatever you see on TikTok is not exactly what happens in Canada.
- The cash value of policies is usually included in the family patrimony.
- Borrowing money from it has normally a higher interest rate than using a line of credit.
- A lot of agents sell it with a catch phrase like " you could borrow from it to give a house cash down for your kids". For the regular people, the cash value never goes high enough to have a cash down on a house.
- Pay 20. This policy means that you pay for 20 years but are covered until death. It is a way to pay your policy faster.

Universal Life insurance
- Almost the same as the insurance above.
- Has an investment part in it.
- There is a calculation that is needed, and you will receive an annual statement telling you how much more you can deposit into your policy. Example: Monthly premium to keep your insurance alive: $100.   Maximum monthly payment $400. (Which means anything above $100 will be an investment.)
- ***If you a not a wealthy individual, but your agent is pushing for this one, run.*** A discussion is required why you would *want* to have this instead of maximising your RRSP and TFSA.
- This type of insurance is perfect for someone who has maximised their RRSP, TFSA, RESP, they opened a Family Trust, and they have so much money they do not know what to do with it. This is a perfect tool to give more money to beneficiaries instead of going through taxes at death.

Accident (injury) insurance

I once met with a woman who had nothing, no insurance, no savings.
Her budget was <u>$100 per month</u> to start some sort of insurance, and
savings, a retirement plan and a RESP for her kids. Impossible?
We did:
- $25 per month accident insurance
- $25 per month RESP
- $50 per month RRSP
- No life insurance because she had a small one through work.
- The plan was to eventually upgrade her protection with time.
- So, it meant, if her salary grew, it was not time to upgrade her house, but look into the important things, like proper coverage.

Accident insurance covers you for the stupid things like falling on ice
and breaking a leg and not being to work for 2 months.
- It does not cover for a disability, like cancer or depression.
- Normally does not have a medical exam.
- Pretty affordable
- A couple of coverage options
- This allows for peace of mind for accidents that can happen outside of work. (Because depending on where you live, we are covered for accidents that happen at work.)

Critical Illness Insurance

Most CI insurance work the same way:

- This covers a main illness like cancer.
- Once you get a diagnostic, you must survive at least 30 days, and then you will receive a lump sum.
- The lump sum you receive is normally not taxable. (if an individual contract that you pay your own premiums)
- The lump sum chosen at underwriting is NOT based on your salary. You have the freedom to purchase the coverage you want.
- You do not have to work to purchase, example, a stay-at-home mom would benefit greatly from a Ci if she got sick.
- Read properly the contract to see what the illnesses (and severity) are covered. Example, the loss of one eye might not be covered, but they will cover 2.   And the first 3 stages of cancer might not be covered.
- Some policies have a huge application and underwriting process, so any claim is supposed to be easier.
- Some policies are cheaper, have less demands at application, but the claims will be harder and might be refused. (do not go for the easier applications unless you really do not have the budget for a good insurance.

You can guess, the total cost of the policy will be greatly affected by the quality of the clauses. Someone with only 4 illnesses will pay much less than someone who has the 25 illnesses. (assuming everything else is the same, in theory).

CI and Di are the types of insurance that have many options. You cannot really compare the cost you pay with your friend's cost. When comparing, you must look at all the details.

Some differences in policies include:
- Sometimes there are only 4 illnesses covered. (example: life-threatening cancer, heart attack, stroke, and coronary bypass surgery)
- Sometimes there are 10 illnesses covered.
- Sometimes there are 25. (Example: Alzheimer's, Parkinson's, MS, benign brain tumor.)
- There might be a refund of premiums at age xx. Meaning, if you continue to pay until age xx, and never do any claim, they will refund your monthly premiums that you have paid.
- There might be 2 events allowed. Meaning: you get a cheque if you have cancer, and then 2 years later for a stroke.
- Level premium, means the monthly cost stays the same
- Level premium 10, means the monthly cost stays the same for the first 10 years.
- Pay 20 to 75.   Means you pay for 20 years but are covered until 75. At 75, you are either no longer covered, or you receive a refund.

Disability insurance

I went over briefly the disability product when discussing the Group Plan above, but here are more details.

- The coverage amount you can apply for is based on your income.
- If you become disabled, it will be a monthly amount that you receive in your bank account. (it is not a lump sum)
- It is meant to replace income; it is not meant to become richer from a disability.
- The cost of the insurance is based on multiple factors, including your job description. For example, an exterior window-washer of high-rise buildings will have a hard time getting insurance, and if they do, it will be expensive.
- Your advisor should always offer you the best protection for your job and show you some cheaper options. If they do not offer you options, speak up, ask questions.

The Disability Insurance is the product that has the most options, and you must understand the differences. The BEST product available for you, for your job description/ category, will be the most expensive.

The best policy I have seen had the following description:
- 30-day waiting period
- No exclusion (besides the 3 main ones)
- Own profession
- Coverage up to age 65.
- Guaranteed, non-cancelable
- Non-taxable
- No integration
- No coordination
- Possibility of prolongation

Waiting period:
The most popular option chosen is the 90-day waiting period, because it is the least expensive.
There is normally the option of 30 days, 60 days, and 90 days.
Important to note: the waiting period is for when the coverage would start, not the exact day you would receive the amount of money in your bank account.

Exclusions:

Most policies will have the 3 main exclusions:

- For a disability due to an act or accident of war, whether declared or undeclared,
- For normal pregnancy or childbirth (but it will cover disabling complications of pregnancy or childbirth, or)
- During any period that you are incarcerated.

AND :

Exclusions will be added on to your policy based on your health history and your job description.   We often see an exclusion for depression for some high-risk jobs.

If you have a history of something they will probably be excluded. Most common are back and mental health issues. (of course, do not lie, because medical files are always checked)

Definition of disability:

Does it cover full Own Profession . It will cover your own profession, or ANY profession.

Meaning, if you're a surgeon, but lose the mobility of your hands, your 'own profession' coverage would pay you.

 'Any profession' would mean that the insurance company would not pay, because you would be able to teach.

Coverage up to age 65.

This is easy to understand. If you have a disability, will the insurance pay you for 2 years, 5 years, up to age 65 .

Of course, up to age 65 will be the most expensive. If you are a highly trained professional, like a doctor, a dentist , etc, you should definitely take the best coverage.

Having a 2-year coverage is better than anything.

Guaranteed, non-cancelable

The non cancelable clause does not mean that YOU cannot cancel. It means that the insurance company cannot cancel.

The guaranteed part is what is important. If it is a guaranteed product, you will not have to fight at a claim .

Non-taxable.

This part is easy to understand. If it is an individual policy that you own, and you pay, the benefit would be non-taxable.

If it is a policy that you got as a benefit, through your business or work, the benefit might be taxable. This makes a difference in your budget.

No Integration.
Depending on where you live, you might be lucky enough to have some sort of coverage from the government.

Integration means that your DI policy would pay you the difference between what you are allowed , minus what you are getting from the government.   You might think it is unfair, but this policy is cheaper than a *no integration* clause.

No coordination
No coordination means that no matter other coverage you have through work or individually, they will not take in into consideration.

Possibility of prolongation
Do we really stop working at age 65 ?   DI coverage normally ends at 65. This might be important for you, to keep a coverage longer than 65. This is not automatic, and you probably have to prove that you are still working past 65. But when you apply for a DI coverage, check if this is a possibility.

Possibility of transformation
What I have seen in the past, that I thought was cool , was the ability to transform the DI insurance into a long-term care insurance.
Long-term care insurance might not exist anymore, it is an insurance that pays to cover your basics needs when you are no longer able to take care of yourself.

Pet insurance

Yes, I want to discuss this. A pet that has a $10,000 vet bill is what can really hurt you financially. Sometimes stupid things happen, like your dog chased a porcupine.

I will not give details here, because I have seen way too many options.

My recommendations:
- Ask your vet which pet insurance they accept and have not seen many issues with.
- Your vet probably already has pamphlets at their desk but have a discussion with the receptionists. They are the ones dealing with the payments, and probably have stories.
- My coverage would not start right away because they wanted to see her medical file before insuring her. (and she had never been to the vet).
    - So, when adopting an animal, make an appointment at the vet for a checkup.
    - Then look into getting insurance.
    - Do not wait until there is a health concern, because exclusions exist in pet insurance as well.
    - Taking insurance when they are young is much cheaper.
    - It gives you peace of mind .
    - If you do not believe in pet insurance, you should definitely have an emergency fund for pets. (which is not the same thing, it takes time to accumulate $10K-$20K)

How much RRSP/TFSA/FHSA room you have (this is found on the CRA web site.)

When talking to clients, I ask what their RRSP/TFSA/FHSA room they have. This is found on your online access with Canada Revenue Agency.

It is important to know these numbers to create a financial plan. If you have no room at all, it means putting more investments into taxable accounts and coming up with a taxation plan. If you have plenty of room in the TFSA and RRSP, we check if/when to maximize those.

The FHSA is a new type of account that we started to open in 2023. It is the First Home Savings Account. This account is for those who are planning to buy a house. Your room depends on when you opened the account. If you opened the account in 2024, you do NOT have the 2023 room of $8000. You must be 18 to open.

Did you open a FHSA in 2023? (or planning to open one?)

When meeting with clients who are currently renting, we ask if they are planning to buy a house. Saving for a cash down might take time, and now we have a tool like the FHSA that is interesting.

Always tell your advisor if you are planning to use a chink of your investments for something like real estate purchases.

Did you receive an inheritance, or think you will receive one?

Thinking that you will receive an inheritance in the future is NOT a retirement plan.

The reason why we ask is about knowing your complete profile. I normally create a financial plan without this number. Once (or if) you inherit, we will adjust your financial plan in consequence.

IF you are not in Canada :

Chapter one was all about knowing your numbers.

Budget and income are the same, no matter where you are.

What do you currently have in place?

Do you have some benefits/ retirement plans/ protection at work?

What does your government offer you if you get sick or disabled?

Chapter two: Control your expenses.

The first step to controlling your expenses is with a monthly budget. Meaning; all expenses for the year divided up between the twelve months. Include everything. Birthday parties, gifts, holidays, snow removal, taxes, dentist, summer trips, clothing and back-to-school spending, and much more.

We reviewed the budget in the previous chapter, and in case you skipped:

Tips and notes:

- The first time you do this, you might feel overwhelmed.
- Being in denial about all the expenses is more common than you think.
- Doing the budget is the first step; you have to be ok with whatever comes up. Accept it and move on. Knowledge is better than being in denial and getting deeper into debt.
- Be realistic about your expenses. Do not put $200 for Christmas if you spend $1500 on gifts and decorations.
- Excel sheets are great, start a new tab for a new year and see your progress throughout the years. Or a personal tab and a business tab.
- Every dollar counts. Try to be as close as possible. For example, do not put $1000 for mortgage payments, if the amount is $1189.90.

The second step is looking at all of the expenses. See if there are any than you can cut. For example, I often hear from women that they do not have money to invest, not even $25 per month. However, they do their nails once a month; go to the hairdresser, etc. No judgement, really.

However. If building wealth is your goal, trying to cut expenses should be your priority.

Expenses that are easily cut:
- Coffee from a coffee shop. With a scone or muffin
- Lunches at work
- Dinners out with friends
- Nails, hair
- Gym memberships that we do not really use.
- $320 Zumba memberships for 8 sessions.
- Clothing and shoes
- $800 per month personal trainers. There are plenty of ways to get in shape without spending $800 a month. And if you are spending $800 a month on a personal trainer, but do not put as much in savings/investing , than you need a serious look at your priorities.
- Lottery tickets. There is a difference between one ticket once in a while, compared to spending $50 a week.
- Quick bite to eat between school and soccer practice.
- Encouraging friends with their home-based business. Go ahead, and help out your friends with their Avon, Tupperware, Doterra, etc. However, decide that you will limit those expenses on a monthly basis, otherwise you might lose control.

Expenses that you could review:

- Interest rates on your credit cards. Contact your bank to see if you can lower your rates or change cards. For example, a card that accumulates points for trips might have a higher interest rate that a simple card.
- Check with your employer if they have deals with home/car insurance, or any other deals.
- Car payments. I often see someone who has $0 savings but has a $900 per month BMW car payment. A car depreciates in value, so do not tell me it is an investment. **Looking** rich does not help you **get** rich. The millionaires I know drive Toyotas and Mazdas. When you are truly rich, you do not want to be bothered by strangers. (buying an expensive car gets you noticed by the wrong people).
- Sometimes people have too much insurance, or the wrong kind. I once met a man who had 5 accident protections, but no life insurance. (He thought it was 5 life insurance policies). Make an appointment with your advisor to review.
- Travel Insurance. Before buying one, check to see if you are covered with your credit card. (Travel insurance coverage when the trip is purchased with the credit card).
- Your housing costs. As mentioned in the chapter before, if your housing, car and groceries are more than 50% of your income, then you made some wrong decision along the way. You do not NEED a house, and especially not the fanciest one you could be approved for. I once met a single woman who decided to rent a brand new place, it was expensive , but "deserved to be in a nice place" . Her rent was $500 more than some other places in the area at that time. $500 a month could have been a nice monthly saving.

Be careful before cutting or reducing:

- Often, the first expenses to be cut are the insurance payments. Life Insurance, Disability, Critical Illness. Do not cancel or modify this without a discussion and analysis from your advisor.
    - Instead of cancelling, check to see if you could reduce the coverage, thus reducing the cost.
    - Check to see if there are cheaper options.
    - If you stopped smoking, check to see if you are eligible for a reduced premium. (after a year of not smoking)
    - For joint policies, especially if you separated or divorced, check to see if it can be separated. (example : joint life insurance . Woman and older man. The woman kept paying the policy as is, until she realised that out of the $80 premium, $55 was for the man. True story)
- Chiro, nutritionist, kine, dermato. Do you really need 2 appointments per week? Do they now offer insurance receipts? Do they offer payment plans ? Taking care of your health is a priority. If you think staying healthy is expensive, imagine getting sick. However, make sure you spend your money wisely, with professionals who are really certified. (nutritionist versus someone who sells protein shakes) .
- Reality check with your MLM. (Multi-Level-Marketing)   Are you really making money, or spending every month, trying to build your downline?
- Same as your business. A budget should also be done for your business, separate from personal. Check if anything that needs to be cut.

If you are not in Canada.

Insurance products are similar no matter which country you are in, and it is often the first thing that people cut when they are struggling financially. Before cancelling any lie or health insurance, talk to an advisor.

Cutting other expenses, like restaurants and expensive coffee trips seem to be the same everywhere.

No matter which country I am in, I could say " stop spending" !

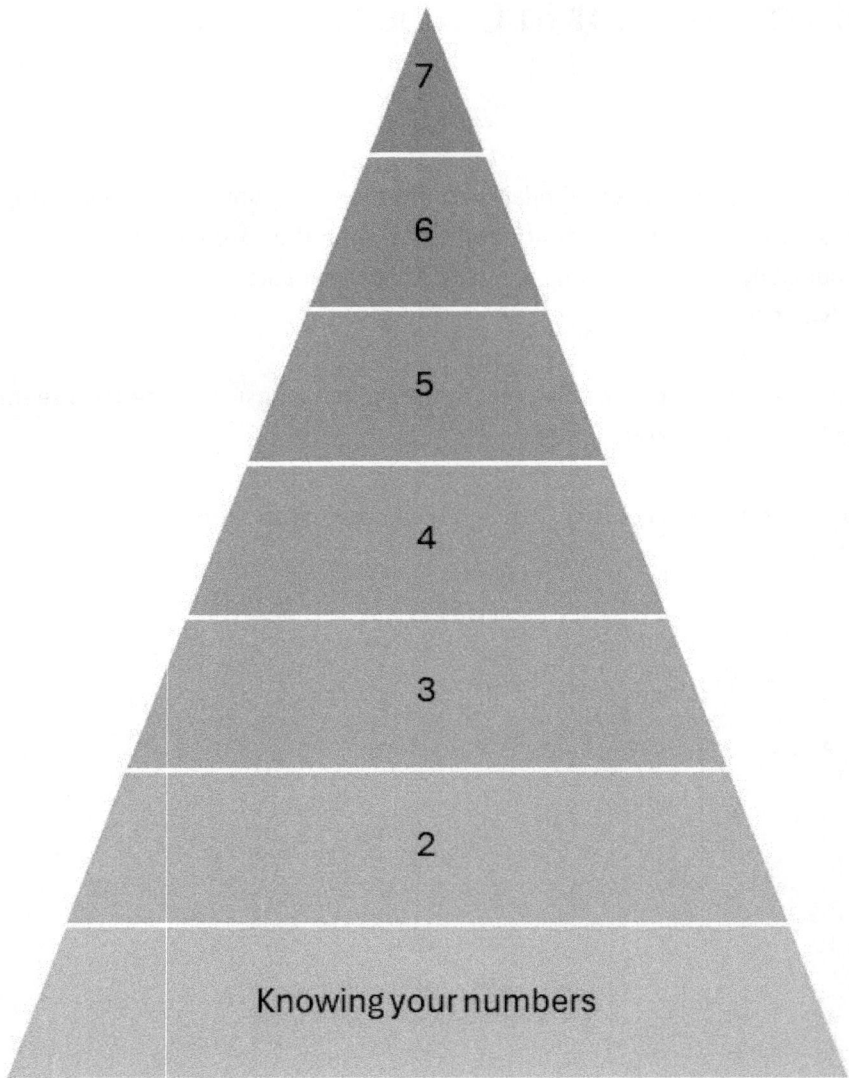

Your financial information and tools

Chapter three: Have the proper advising team.

The stats in Canada are still astounding. Only one in four are currently saving enough money for retirement. And out of those people, 85% have an advisor. So then, it means that people who work closely with an advisor have a better financial / retirement plan.

How to choose the proper financial advising team? Where to go? There are a couple of options opened to you.

1) Simply open a retirement account with your current bank.

Advantages:

- You already have accounts with your bank, so opening another is easy.
- You probably have access to the app or site, so it is convenient.
- You can open an account with $0, and start contributing the amount you wish, as little as $25 per month.
- They might offer you a discussion with an advisor and prepare a financial plan.
- For most of the population, having savings and investment accounts with the bank is sufficient.
- When you have reached a certain level on investments, they will recommend that you meet with a private banker, or an investment advisor.

Disadvantages:

- Not an advisor that you can text on a Sunday night with a quick question regarding your TFSA.
- Bank employees come and go, no real relationship is built.
- You can deal with the bank for 25 years, come in one day and no one knows your name, or appreciate how loyal you have been to them.
- Unless you have reached a certain level of investments, you do not have access to an Investment Advisor nor a Private banker. Those are for the High Net Worth individuals only. You might

feel less important to the bank than your neighbor who has more money.

- These might not seem like real disadvantages, but I have nothing bad to say about banks. They serve a purpose; I like getting my paycheque deposited in my account. I like being able to pay my bills, and transfer money.

2) Financial Security Advisor.

A financial security advisor can help you with things that the bank employees cannot. The reason? Different licenses and regulations. A financial Security Advisor has an insurance license. Their goal is to meet with a prospect, and go over their financial situation, including insurance and savings.

Advantages:

- They work for free, with the hope that you will become a client. (often, they do not have a base salary, they only receive commission)
- They have access to financial planning software
- They will ask you if you have a Will and Mandate
- They will ask you if you are common-law or married (and might start a discussion about the difference and your rights)
- They will explain Life Insurance, Disability, Critical Illness
- They will go over your coverage at work.

- They can open investment accounts for you, also with $0 and a small monthly contribution.
- Service is personalised.
- Some even give you their cell number, so you can text them with any crazy question.
- They will remember your birthday and will care if your cat dies.
- A go-to person if you urgently need the service of another professional (notary, lawyer, etc.)

Disadvantages:

- Insurance reps still have a bad reputation in our minds, the insurance pusher, similar to the vacuum vendor from the 80's.
- Almost seems like firms recruit daily, (feels like they recruit almost anyone, get the family members as clients, and move on to the next kid they can hire.)
- Reps from a certain firm want to sell you insurance and want to recruit you at the same time. It is a weird conversation. It almost feels like they make more money recruiting than selling insurance. (not naming the firm, you can guess)
- You can clearly see that some reps are in this for the commission, and not for the love of the career. It is too bad; they are ruining it for the good ones.
- There is such a high turn-over, that you might get a 'new' advisor every 6 months. Each of them will call you and tell you they need to meet.

Since I genuinely believe in the importance of insurance (life, disability, and critical illness), and investing, I strongly recommend a meeting. Meeting an advisor, you can trust. Ask around, you do not have to pick the first one you meet.

3) Private Banker

Once you have reached a certain level of investments & net worth, the cashier at the bank will recommend that you meet wit a Private Banker.

Each private bank is different and offer a variety of services, but here are some examples:

- Skip the lines at the bank. Your private banker can be reached by fax, email, or phone.
- Thorough review of your Wealth management, Estate planning, & retirement needs
- Access to exclusive credit cards and perks, like the loge at the airport.
- Higher daily cash withdrawal limits
- A wide variety of fixed-rate term loan borrowing options.
- Access to short-term cash management through their Treasury Unit.

Some private bankers are more like a concierge service. Contact them to send a cheque to your car dealership or pay your bills, but your investments stay with a securities division. However, some private banks are also after your investment portfolio, and here are the disadvantages:

- Some Private Banking only offer investments of one Mutual Fund company. No diversification, no Stocks, no ETF's.
- Sometimes the fees for Private banking are much higher than accounts with an Investment Advisor, who has access to all investments.

4) Direct trading apps.
- There is no advisor/client relationship with this option.
- You do your own trades, make your own decisions.
- Good for the person who follows the Stock Markets and understands enough to do it themselves.
- There is fee for every transaction done., example: $9.95. (now most apps say that they do not have a trading fee, but you know they get paid somehow, probably through a spread) .
- You are completely on your own when it comes to , well, EVERYTHING finance-related . Have a questions about insurance, financial planning, retirement planning, estates, credit, insurance, etc ? , you are on your own.
- Do not use trading apps unless you know 100% what you are doing.

5) Investment Advisor.

Many years ago, Investment Advisors were referred to as "Stock Brokers". Most of their day was doing transactions and calling their clients to do recommendations. An interesting research called the Brinson study (started in 1974 and lasted for 20 years) showed that 93.6% of the success of a portfolio is with the proper asset allocation (not stock picking, nor trying to time the market) . I read an article about this when I started in this field. It made me laugh, because we all know at least one investment advisor who will contact his clients and gloat about his high returns but will put the blame somewhere else when the markets crash. Today, most advisors that I have met understand this. Trying to 'beat the market', or doing 'market timing' is no longer part of portfolio management nor Wealth Management.

What matters? Making sure you know your client. Their financial goals, their **risk tolerance**, **horizon**. The risk tolerance is normally done through a questionnaire. It aims to find your true tolerance. We still often get this sentence:

 'I want to make money, get a really high return, but do not lose money' .

 Sometimes the person has a fear of the Stock markets (we all know someone who put money in a speculative stock and lost, BreX , for example) .

The main categories are conservative, balanced, and aggressive.

A horizon means in how many years do you need part or all your money. Be truthful with your advisor. You will want to withdraw $30K from your RRSP to purchase your first home? Tell the truth. This will change the investment recommendations.

Investment Advisor do not all work in a bank, but each bank has a securities division, like TD Waterhouse, CIBC Wood Gundy, RBC Dominion Securities (just to give examples, not a list of the best ones) . Investment Advisors have access to almost all types of investments you would want to buy; GIC's, mutual funds, stocks, ETF's, options, seg funds, PPN's, etc.

You can open many types of accounts with them; RRSP, RESP, TFSA, LIRA, RRIF, FHSA etc, and there are 3 main types of fees:

1) Commission account: good for the people who have less than $200K in investments. The account has a yearly fee (RSP $150 per year, for example). A stock or GIC transaction will incur a commission, most of the time it is at least $150. That is why most of these accounts have mutual funds. (no transaction fee)

2) Fee-based: pay an annual fee, normally 1-2% of the value of your portfolio. No fee for individual transactions, with a maximum number of transactions allowed.

3) Discretionary fee based.   Annual fee, but the advisor does not have to contact you to discuss the recommended transactions. Not every advisor can be discretionary, the CIM® title is required. (otherwise, the advisor must contact every client before making the trade). Discretionary transactions means that the client must trust the advisor and has to sign an agreement. It also means that the advisor can make one transaction instead of hundreds. For example, the advisor has 100 clients who own Tesla shares. He/she believes that it is time to sell 25 % of the portfolio. Without the CIM® license, he/she would have to call the 100 clients to discuss and get the approval for this change How many hours will it take to contact 100 clients ? Discretionary trading means one simple transaction. No phone calls.

Not every firm has the technology/ compliance staff to allow for discretionary platforms, and there are still many advisors who are not licensed. Most High Net Worth clients ($1 million or more of investable assets) want to be in discretionary.

The investment advisor is often limited to the type of clients they can take. Each firm has their minimum accounts. For example, some firms will allow the opening of smaller accounts, but the advisor will not be paid on those accounts below $100K.

Then, the advisor must decide if they really want to put the time/ effort in keeping those accounts. Often, we still do. Especially if that smaller account is the child of an important client, or the account has the potential to grow since the client is a law student.

How do you decide where and with whom you want to invest your money?   A financial security advisor? Simply at the bank? Or with an Investment Advisor?   You could always leave it with the bank until you meet the advisor who you feel a connection with.

Choosing an advisor is no longer about who impresses you with big words, or who seems to have the most confidence. Arrogance no longer has room. People want to feel empowered and taken care of at the same time. They want to feel that the advisor understands their needs and have really listened. Chose the advisor who cares about you and your family. Did the advisor ask you the following questions:

- Do you have elderly parents to take care of (or in the future)?
- Do you have Wills and mandates (and are they up to date) ?
- Do you have personal insurance and/or at work?
- Any disabled child or dependent?
- Have you ever invested in the market before?
- How do you dream your retirement will be like ?
- Etc..

There are questions to get to know you more and understand your situation. Investment advisors do much more than just give investment recommendations. Investment advisors can help you with :

- Retirement planning
- Estate planning
- Business succession planning
- Philanthropy
- Risk management through insurance
- Budgeting
- Educational plan
- Etc.

The trick to finding a good financial advisor:

- Learn the types of financial advisors in your area.
- If you have a decent amount of investable assets, go for the advisors who have licenses to trade stocks.
- If you are just starting out, you can stick with the bank you are already at.
- If you want to have a little bit of guidance, and have little money, go with the advisor with the insurance licence.
- Of course, ask friends and family who they trust with their money. But what if you are the only person in your entourage that has money? Meet up with richer friends and ask them. There is a huge difference between all those types of advisors, especially when it comes to knowledge, expertise, and access to investments.
- Meet with the advisor and ask questions. You must feel comfortable with them.
- Meet more than one to compare.
- When you meet the right one, you will feel it.
- Do NOT use the same advisor as your spouse if the advisor treats you like you are just the wife, with no opinion. I have seen it too many times, where the male advisor talks to the male client, and ignores the wife. Made me want to do conferences for women.

If you are not in Canada:

- Find out the main types of financial advisors there are in your area.
- What are the licensing requirements?
- If they work in Investments, they should have some sort of licensing requirements to trade on the Stock Markets.
- If they sell insurance, there are probably licensing requirements as well.

If you have no clue how to check, make a list of your family or friends that you could have a discussion with, and write down your questions:

Chapter Four

Understanding inflation and how it affects your wealth.

You probably already understand inflation.

The raising cost of things we buy.

The terms "cost of living' and 'inflation" are often interchanged in conversations but are not quite the same things. The cost of living in Toronto is higher than in Montreal. The difference in the cost of living in cities/provinces is mainly because of housing, employment, taxes. The inflation rate for Canada is at an average of 2% per year.

Why is it important to understand inflation and the cost of living? To help us make smarter choices when it comes to employment and investments.

<u>Employment :</u>

Let's say you have applied for different positions. One of them the starting salary is a little higher. However, they do not give yearly raises (and people seem to have to beg for raises) The other company gives a 3% raise every year. This would be a simple choice, go with the company that gives 3% raises. (Otherwise, every year, while your salary stays the same, the cost of living goes up. Every year your salary has less buying power, thus you become 'poorer' as the years go by), If you intend to switch jobs every year, I guess it does not matter. Imagine if you would stay with that company for 10 years. How much lower will your salary be compared to the peers working for the competition?

Loyalty to your company that you love is great but imagine finding out that employees at a competing firm makes a lot more money than you. Knowledge is key. Be curious about how much you are worth.

Also, what if you are asked to move to another province, for work. They offer to refund travelling expenses, great. But what about a raise? If you go from Montreal to Toronto, without a significant raise in your salary, (to cover the difference in the cost of living) would that be wise?

Investments:

Wouldn't it be great if we could invest our money, make a huge return, but with no risk at all?

That would be great. However, we all know that the greater the risk, the greater the possibility of the reward. Some people have lost a lot of money investing in the market, (for many difference reasons, like investing in very speculative stocks, or putting all of their money in a single stock, because they believed they hit a jackpot). The fear of investing in the stock market might be keeping you poor.

Some people, because of this fear, invest only in GIC's. (guaranteed investment certificate).

Features:

- This investment is 100% guaranteed.
- Has a maturity, example 1 year, 2 years, etc.)
- Most of the time: your money is locked-in, cannot redeem the GIC before maturity.
- The rate is known in advance, example: 1.5%

You might understand then, that GIC's do not protect your money from inflation, when the rates are low like they have been in the past many years. This is an investment of choice for the elderly, who have worked hard in saving and investing, but can no longer afford risk.

If you are saving for retirement, and want your money to grow, GIC's are probably not your first choice.

When we do retirement projections, we often use the inflation rate of 2-3%, and an average investment return of 6%.   I have seen some advisors use returns of 8-12% or more in their retirement plans, (to make it look as though you need to save less for retirement). **Returns (unless in GIC's) are never guaranteed.** Be wary if approached by someone who guarantees an incredible return.

Your investments will grow every year if your returns beat inflation. How much you will be able to accumulate, and how fast your money grows depends on your willingness to take risk.

Chapter Five

Understanding the magic of compounding interest

The word interest makes you think of credit card debts or your investments. Interest, especially compounded, can either help you build wealth, or can destroy you.

I come from a poor family. When I was 12 years old, the word interest was confusing to me. I thought **interest** was bad:

- "my interest rate is killing me'
- "my interest amount is too high, I have trouble paying it"

But then, I heard someone say:

"I am glad I received my interest today in my bank account."

I do not remember exactly when I understood ***that interest is paid on amounts borrowed:***

- **You** borrow from a credit card, **you** pay interest.
- The bank borrows money from you (through a GIC for example), the bank owes you interest.

Learning about investments changed my life. I was 12 and wanted to buy shares of Pepsi.

Interest is neither bad nor good. Credit cards are useful but can destroy our credit if misused.

Compounding interest is simply: interest on interest.

- 2% interest on 100$ becomes $102.
- Then; 2% on $102, (not $100), thus $104.04

Compounding interest is the secret to building wealth, with time and patience. Why is this interesting? It is interesting when you see how little money it takes to build wealth over a long period (thus starting to invest at 18 years old instead of 50)

Consider the rule of 72 to figure out how many years it takes to double your money.

72 divided by the **investment return** is the amount of years it takes to double your money.

For example :

Invested in a GIC at 1.5% : Your $10K invested will become **$20K** in 48 years.   (72/1.5 = 48, therefore takes 48 years to double)

Your $10K invested at 6% will become $**160K** in 48 years. (doubles every 12 years)

Your $10K invested at 12% will become **$2.5 million** in 48 years. (doubles every 6 years).

Would you rather take zero risk (by buying a GIC with that $10K at 18 years old) , or build a bigger portfolio ?

Rule of 72

Years	1,50%	3%	6%	12%
0	10 000,00 $	10 000,00 $	10 000,00 $	10 000,00 $
6				20 000,00 $
12			20 000,00 $	40 000,00 $
18				80 000,00 $
24		20 000,00 $	40 000,00 $	160 000,00 $
30				320 000,00 $
36			80 000,00 $	640 000,00 $
42				1 280 000,00 $
48	20 000,00 $	40 000,00 $	160 000,00 $	2 560 000,00 $

Would you rather have $20,000 at retirement or $2.5Million?

Of course, 12% returns are never guaranteed.

Even if you know that investments do not have a guaranteed return, would you take the risk to invest in Stocks or Mutual Funds, now that you understand this?

Imagine an 18-year old who invests $10K, in either mutual funds or stocks, and simply forgets it for 48 years until their retirement. Now, instead, imagine trying to start saving at 50 years old.

The secret is the magic of compounded interest. (Albert Einstein called this the 8th wonder of the world) . Starting young, investing even a little, can grow to a lot over many years.

Therefore, this is the reason there are people you know who seem to have accumulated much more wealth for retirement than others. Maybe they simply saved more, maybe they invested well.

If you are not in Canada:

Inflation and interest are the same no matter where you are.

Find out if there are investments that have a guaranteed return. (I mean products from banks or other financial institutions, do not ask your brother-in-law, or the guy that just opened up a corner office)

Make a list of types of investments in your area that are considered low risk, medium risk and high risk.

Low : something that has capital guarantees.

Medium, like a mutual fund, or a blue-chip stock

High risk: speculative stocks

Chapter Six

Stocks

What is a stock ? (also known as having equity in a
company)   A **stock** is ownership of a fraction of a corporation.

For example, you can own shares, or stocks of, Royal bank, Dollarama,
Pepsi, Starbucks, Apple, Tesla, McDonald's to name a few (not a
recommendation, just examples).   These are public companies, their
shares available to purchase, and sell on Stock markets like on the TSX,
Toronto Stock Exchange, in Canada, or on the NYSE.

Like I mentioned, at 12 I was intrigued by Stocks, especially stories of
tremendous wealth gained by individuals. (back then it was the Pepsi
story, today is the Apple or Tesla stories. People building tremendous
wealth by taking a chance, and risk, on a stock they believed in) . Of
course, I would never recommend investing all your money on a single
stock.

I was 12, and wanted to buy something, anything. I was thinking "buy and hold", even at this age.

I was told only adults can make investments, and only the rich have access to Investment Advisors. (no apps back then , it seemed like an untouchable thing for me)

When I was in college, there were guys in my class who seem to be getting rich with a Stock called Bre-X. (rich on paper only of course) That stock seemed to be going up at a tremendous rate). They came to school everyday bragging about how the stock was going up.   Turns out Bre-X was a scam. (and I think they lost all of their money)

I was curious;
- how were they able to buy stocks?
- Do they personally know an Investment Advisor?
- and if so, why did he/she let them buy something so speculative?
- Who told them to buy into that?
- And why they did not sell when it was going up? (make a quick profit since it was a speculation anyways, not a good stock to buy and hold)

Now that I have been in this field for 19 years, I am hoping those guys were not turned off to the idea of investments. Buying into a speculative stock is a huge risk, and betting all your money on something so speculative is gambling.

How, when and where to buy stocks ?

- Stocks can be purchased through an **Investment Advisor** in a securities firm , or simply through a trading app. (vive la technologie) . Investment advisors have licenses to trade securities. The licenses are obtained by CSI, Canadian Securities Institute. (in Canada).
- The TSX in Canada (the NYSE and NASDAQ in the USA) are open from 9;30 to 4pm Eastern Standard Time.
- You can buy/sell "at market" which means you will get the price currently trading at
- If there is low volume (means the price can dramatically go up or down), you might want to control your buying/selling price by entering a specific price
- Decide on the stock you want to buy, and know its current price. For example, each share is how much ? If you have $1000 to invest, but each share is $1000, you will buy only 1 share (not calculating commission).
- If you have an Investment Advisor, simply ask him/her about buying the stock you are hoping to invest in. There will be a conversation about the suitability of the stock in your portfolio.

Why buy stocks?   As seen in previous chapters, leaving your money uninvested does not protect you from inflation. Investing in no-risk GIC's might not give you the returns necessary to build a retirement fund. Your biggest risk is **not** a short-time loss or monthly fluctuations. ***Your biggest risk is not accumulating enough money for retirement.***

There will always be stories of people losing money in the Stock Markets, but the lesson you should learn is not that investing is too risky. You must understand the difference between gambling and investing.

Gambling is like:
- listening to your brother-in-law who says he got a tip from a friend to buy a certain stock , and that it will go through the roof soon.
- Buying into a penny stock because you saw a post on Social media
- Buying into a new Crypto currency that keeps going up because all your friends made money and you feel left out.
- Reading an interesting news article about a public company and thinking that you found a winner.

The secret to investing is :

- Understand that there are fluctuations in the markets
- If your investments are keeping you up at night, it means that you took too much risk
- Building a portfolio does not mean putting all your money in Stocks
- Market timing, trying to beat the market, is **not** the key to high return.
- Asset Allocation is 96.3% of the long-term success of building wealth
- Asset Allocation is deciding how much is invested in stocks and fixed income (example a 70-30 portfolio means 70% is invested in Stocks, 30% in GIC's and other conservative fixed-income investments)
- Invest in stocks you believe in, that you feel are here to stay and have the potential to keep growing.
- Some people invest only in dividend stocks (companies give you dividends, money, for simply holding the stock)
- Diversify means not putting all your money in a single stock or sector. (example, it would not be smart to have a portfolio with only tech stocks like Apple, Paypal, Google and GoDaddy).

- Main stock sectors are : energy, materials, industrials, consumer discretionary, consumer staples, health care, financials, information technology, telecommunications, utilities, real estate.

Think about stocks that you would like to hold; Starbucks , Apple, Google, Salesforce, Royal Bank, Nike, Yahoo, Walt Disney, Procter & Gamble, Air Canada, Tesla, ZOOM, Amazon, Sony, etc. (this is not a recommended list, just names you know) If you have mutual funds, your mutual funds might have these as their top holdings. A great way to invest in the Stock Market when we have a little bit of money is through mutual funds, explained in the next chapter.

"Do not put all of your money on one basket" does NOT mean open many different accounts!

Chapter Seven

Mutual funds

What is a mutual fund?

- It is an investment tool.
- Your money is pooled with other people's money.
- That money is kept with a portfolio manager
- His/her job is to invest in stocks, GIC's, etc, for everyone in the pool
- The name of the mutual fund indicates what the investments will be
- Example: A **Canadian dividend mutual fund** will have investments in Canadian public companies who distribute dividends.
- Example: an **American growth fund** will have American companies that are suspected to grow. (the emphasis is not on the dividends, but on the growth)
- Example: **Canadian Bond fund** will have conservative investments in bonds.
- You can invest as little as $25 per month with some funds

- You can buy/sell at any moment (takes 2 days to settle)
- The fund might be low risk, medium or high risk
- You hold units of the mutual funds, not the actual shares of the companies it is invested in.
- It allows you to have investments with very little deposits
- Banks and other financial institutions offer mutual funds
- Can be held in any type of accounts; RRSP, TFSA, cash, RESP, LIRA, etc.

You can read the mutual fund document, called the **fund fact**, to know the following :

- Date it started
- How much total assets invested in the fund
- Minimum investment required (some mutual funds require $500, $1000 etc)
- Top ten holdings
- Investment mix (which sectors)
- Risk rating
- Returns of current and past years.
- The name of the portfolio manager

<u>It is a MYTH that to become rich you must invest only in individual Stocks.</u>

Mutual funds invest in stocks, so technically people are right.

But **YOU** do not have to invest ONLY in stocks if you want to build wealth. Mutual funds are a great way to start off. Once you reach a certain level of wealth, let's say $150K or more of invested money, diversification is important.

Why not stay in mutual funds, no matter how much money you have?

Because,

- if you have a lot of money, and invest in 20-30 different mutual funds, EACH mutual fund might invest in the same stocks. Take a look at 10 different American fund, they probably all hold the same top 10 , like Amazon, Tesla, Microsoft ? (just a list , not a recommendation)
- Diversification is then not achieved.
- High Net Worth individuals often deal with Investment Advisors, CIM , and hold a combination stocks, bonds and mutual funds. What we often see is holding CAD and USA stocks , but mutual funds that invest globally.
- Do not let anyone tell you that mutual funds are not good.
- Once you have enough wealth, talk to an advisor about moving on to individual stocks.

Other tips:

- Most banks, in Canada, have their own mutual funds that they will offer you in your accounts with them.
- The advisor, as the bank, often does not know more about investments than what they have in their firm.
- They are not licensed to trade Stocks or ETFs, and the bank cannot offer you that.
- The advisor will make you answer a risk profile questionnaire to see how much risk you are willing to take. This is a tricky part. The questionnaire is great, but also have a discussion. If you are too scared of risk, your profile will be conservative. A conservative profile normally generates about 2% returns. Is really that what you want? Let's say you have 20 years before retirement, you want your money to stay the same. (2% return, but there is a 2% inflation, so no growth, really) . I am telling you to go aggressive growth, I am just telling you to have a logical conversation about your time horizon (In how many years you will need the money).

Chapter Eight

Fixed Income

To understand the term Fixed-Income, think of it this way.

- It is when we lend money to a bank, a corporation, or municipality.
- We know exactly how much interest, or income, we will receive.
- Interest is fixed at purchase.
- Term is fixed at purchase.

The most common ones we see in Canada are:

- GIC's (Guaranteed Investment Certificate)
- Money Market
- Bonds

Here are general details of GIC's:

- Principal is protected.
- Protection comes from the Canada Deposit Insurance Corporation, up to $100K per member.
- There is a minimum investing amount (some have as little as $500)
- Term: your money is locked-in for the term. (unless it is a cashable GIC). Terms can be from a few months to several years. The most popular are 1, 2,3,4 and 5 years.
- Interest rate. Rates vary depending on many factors. As we have seen since covid, interest rates went up.
- Types of GIC's. cashable and non-cashable. There might be more available, like a foreign currency GIC.
- Benefits include safety.
- Drawback includes money might be locked-in, which you knew going in, but suddenly needing money. And possibility of low interest rates that do not even cover inflation.
- You can hold GIC's in every type of account (depending on where your accounts are.)
- An Investment Advisor has access to many different ones.
- Banks offer their own GIC's only.

Here are general details of Money Market:

- Perfect for short-term investing
- Basically, IOUs issued by government, financial institutions, or large corporations.
- Very liquid
- Many consider money market as extraordinarily safe.
- Trades in T+1 (meaning I sell today, the money is available tomorrow. Compared to stocks which are now T+2)
- It is not a chequing or savings account; it is a mutual fund.

Bond

Similar to a GIC

- The initial price of most bonds is set at par, or at a face value with increments of $1000. The face value is what you will receive at maturity.
- The actual market price, or what you actually pay for it, of the bond depends on a couple of factors :
  - The current interest rate environment. If interest rates go up in the market, the value of your current bond will go down.
  - The credit quality of the issuer.

- The market value of your bond will fluctuate, and you might notice it on your account statement. The market value shows you how much you could get for it if you sold it, it does not represent how much money you will get at maturity.

- The coupon rate is affected by the current rates, but it is also correlated to the issuer's credit rating. If the issuer has a bad credit rating, they have to offer a higher interest rate to get investors.
- Coupon dates are the dates that the bond issuer will make payments.
- Maturity date is the date that the bond matures and that you will receive back the face value of the bond. (So, if you purchase the bond BELOW the face value, you are not getting back what you paid, you are getting back the face value. Meaning if you bought a bond at 990$, but its face value is $1000, you will get $1000 at maturity.)
- Credit ratings are important to understand, because you do NOT choose a bond based solely on the interest rate.
    - There are 3 main American rating agencies that evaluate the creditworthiness of bonds: Moody's, S&P and Fitch.
    - In Canada, there is Morningstar DBRS.
    - An example of a rating, from the BEST to the "non-investment grade" : AAA, AA+, AA, AA-, A+, A, A-, BBB+, BBB, BBB- …… D

Since bonds are a little bit complicated to understand, I personally have seen more people buying GIC's. (you know exactly the maturity date and the interest rate at purchase).

Chapter Nine

Registered Accounts

(RRSP, TFSA, etc)

I will give you the basic information about the registered accounts. Do not let anyone tell you that one type of account is better than the next. They are all useful. When I talk to a client, analyse their situation, and come up with a plan, it is based on *their* situation. Sometimes we suggest the TFSA over the RRSP, this does NOT mean that you go tell your sister that that is the best solution for *her.*

Registered accounts are given the tax-deferred or tax-sheltered status from the government. The government keeps track of your contributions, withdrawals, and sets rules and regulations that financial institutions have to follow.

- RRSP: Registered Retirement Savings Plan
- LIRA: Locked-in retirement account
- TFSA: Tax-free savings account
- FHSA: First Home Savings Account
- IPP: Individual Pension Plan
- RRIF: Registered Retirement Income Fund
- LIF: Life Income Fund
- RESP: Registered Education Savings Plan
- RDSP: Registered Disability Plan.

A non-registered account, or cash account, is a fully taxable account, you will pay income taxes on interest, dividends or capital losses. You can hold **penny stocks** in a non-registered account, but not in registered accounts.

RRSP

Setting up the RRSP:

- You can open a RRSP through a financial institution, such as a bank, a credit union, or an insurance company.
- The investment you hold inside will depend ENTIRELY on what that institution is allowed to offer. An insurance company will offer you Segregated funds. (similar to mutual funds, but with higher MER's and some sort of guarantee at death and/or maturity). An account with an investment firm will allow you to hold Stocks, ETF's, mutual funds, etc.
- You could set up a regular RRSP, or a spousal. A spousal RRSP means you are the owner of the RRSP, the contributor is your spouse, and the tax receipts go to your spouse. There is a tax issue if there is a withdrawal within 2 years of the contribution.
- Since covid, plenty of firms have made it easy to open accounts online, by virtual appointments, and even using electronic signatures.
-

Contributing to the RRSP:

- Most firms make it possible for the contributions to be taken out of your bank account, with weekly, monthly, and bi-weekly options.
- Automatic purchases of mutual funds (often called PAC's) can often be done as little as $25 per month. ($25 a month is not enough to build wealth, but it is a start)

- Contributions can be regular or spousal. (meaning if you contribute to your spouse's RRSP, you get the tax slip, but the account is in their name)
- If you are an immigrant, you can start contributing to a RRSP the year following your first income tax return. (and of course, verify this info with an accountant, or Revenue Canada directly)
- Everyone's contribution room is different, it is calculated as follows:
    - Unused room from last year
    - **Plus 18% of your earned income for the previous year**.
    - (But do not go over the year's maximum. The 2023 annual limit is $30,780)
    - There is also a calculation with your *pension adjustment*, plus any *pension adjustment reversal*, *minus net past service pension adjustment.*
    - The best way to know where you are at is to check the Revenu Canada website. If you have a Group RRSP or Pension Plan, be aware that you might not be able to contribute 18% in an individual RRSP.
- Over-contributions are penalised at 1% per month.
- Very important: if you are an entrepreneur and pay yourself dividends, it does NOT give you RRSP room.

- Technically, if you work, (a legally declared work) you can open a RRSP, but I have never seen a 16-year-old open a RRSP. Anyone below 18 cannot invest. (so, if you are able to open for a 16year-old, the account will stay in cash...? Again, I have never seen one, and would not necessarily recommend it)
- The contributions to a RRSP are tax deductible.
- You have a $2000 lifetime buffer to over-contribute.
- You can carry-forward RRSP contributions that you did not claim (this means you contribute, invest, but use the deduction later when your income is higher and needs more deductions)
- You cannot claim a tax deduction for:
  - Capital losses.
  - Any admin fees or brokerage fees. (if the advisor tells you to pay the charges from a non-registered account to be able to deduct, RUN. This is false information, and plenty of people got caught about 15 years ago doing this. So, if the advisor is saying this, they have not kept up with their regulations.)
  - Any interest you paid on money borrowed to contribute.
  - Employer contributions
- What does not count as a contribution?
  - If you have money sitting in the RRSP and you decide to invest. Investing it or rebalancing a RRSP account is not a new contribution.
  - A transfer from a RRSP to another RRSP
  - When you put money in your RRSP to pay you're your Home Buyer's Plan or LifeLong Learning Plan.

Transferring to another institution:

- You cannot simply withdraw your RRSP to then deposit it to another firm. Be careful when asking a firm to do a transfer. A transfer is easy, no tax implication. Some have made a mistake by asking a "withdrawal'. Make sure you use the right term. A withdrawal had tax consequences, (seen below).
- If you want to transfer to another firm, there is a form to complete and sign with the institution that will receive the account. They will take care of the transfer.
- Most firms charge to transfer-out a RRSP. The fee can range from $50 to $200 per account.
- Sometimes it is hard to transfer because of how the account is invested in. If you try to move a RRSP that holds stocks to a bank, you will not be able to, without selling.
- Some advisors invest in funds that have fees when you sell them too early. They include Segregated funds, and mutual funds with deferred sales charges. The advisors use these because they make more money from them, or it is a way to keep the client stuck with you. We are not allowed to sell the funds with the Deferred Sales Charges (DSC) anymore, but I still see them in people's account statements. Therefore, if you want to transfer your account from an insurance agent, (who does only seg funds), to an Investment Advisor, there might be some funds that will have fees to get out of.

Making withdrawals tax-free

A RRSP is a great tool to save for retirement. The money gives you a tax deduction and it grows tax-free until retirement.

You can, however, withdraw with no tax consequences for :

- A purchase of your first home, with the Home Buyer's Plan
- Full-time training for you or your spouse

Home Buyer's Plan:

- Do NOT use it to buy Real Estate investment. You might lie and get away with it at first, but the government checks.
- There is a form to fill our and sign, once you know the address of the home you are buying. Do not lie on the form. If you do not qualify, move on.
- It is to buy your first home.
- If you had a home in the past, but then moved into a rental for at least 4 years, you could qualify. (as long as you do not have a HBP balance from the previous home.)
- All you have to do is tell your advisor that you will be buying a home shortly and will do a RRSP withdrawal through the HBP. Do NOT tell them at the last minute. Some firms request a 30-day notice. The RRSP contribution has to be in the account at least 90 days to be able to withdraw.
- You can withdraw up to $35K from your RRSP
- You have 15 years to pay it back, no interest. Be careful how much you withdraw, it might be hard for you to pay it back.
- Paying it back is simple, just deposit money in your RRSP. At tax-time, decide how much is a regular contribution and how much of it is to pay back the HBP.

- There are much more details to know about the HBP, and the best way is to check the HBP page on Revenue Canada's website.

The Lifelong Learning Plan

I personally have never been asked by a client to do this.

- It allows you to withdraw up to $10K in a calendar year to finance full-time training. Up to $20K (so 2 calendar years)
- For you or your spouse, you cannot withdraw for your kids' education.
- The educational program has to be approved by RCA
- You have 10 years to pay back
- If you become a non-resident, or turn 71, you have to pay back faster.
- This is the basic information, and of courser , there is more on the RCA website.

Making taxable withdrawals

Withdrawing money because you have an emergency is possible, but it will be taxed at withdrawal **AND** this will be included in your yearly income.

The tax rates are: (in Quebec, tax rates are different)

- 10% on amounts up to $5,000
- 20% on amounts of $5,000 and over, up to and including $15,000
- 30% on amounts over $15,000

The taxes withheld might not be enough, based on your tax bracket, you may have to pay more tax on the withdrawal when you include it as income in your tax return.

What happens at retirement?

- Do not confuse YOUR day of retirement and the RRSP's maturity.
- Unless you tell your advisor, they do not know when to start giving you retirement income from the RRSP.
- An Investment Advisor does so much more than investing in stocks for you. One of the things we do is to plan your retirement, and look at the tax implications of withdrawing from your different types of accounts. A discussion is required about your RRSP.

- The RRSP **MUST** be converted or withdrawn before December 31st they year that you turn 71. Here are your options:
    - Withdrawing it all as a lump sum. Not recommended unless it is a small account. This amount is added to your yearly income of the year of withdrawal. For most people who have accumulated wealth, this is not even an option that they will consider.
    - Buying an annuity.
        - With the current interest rates, I have not sold any annuities for many years.
        - Annuities may offer a guaranteed income for life or a special time. The details of annuities are varied, you should discuss with an advisor.
        - Income is taxable.
        - The cons are:
            - You do NOT have control of your investments.
            - If you had investments that you had all your life in the RRSP, you cannot transfer those to the annuity. Everything will be sold.
            - Depending on the annuity you get, some annuity payments STOP if you die. The balance is not given to your beneficiaries.

- Converting your RRSP to a RIF
  - This is the most popular option.
  - You convert the year that you want. The year after, you start receiving payments, with a minimum that MUST be taken out.
  - There is a minimum amount to be taken out every year, but no maximum.
  - Payments are taxable.
  - The minimum is based on a ratio set by Revenue Canada. It is based on your age and the market value of your account as of December 31st of the previous year. This means that your minimum payments vary from year to year.
  - You can ask your advisor to give you a specific amount per month. Most advisors can do Ad Hoc payments, and automatic monthly & yearly payments.
  - The payments can be sent directly in your bank account, or it can be kept with the advisor in another account, like the TFSA.
  - For the wealthy individuals who do not need/want their minimum payments, they ask their advisors to transfer them to their TFSA. (RIF payment to the non-registered account, to then be contributed to the TFSA.

What happens at death?

- If the deceased was a participant of a **Home Buyer's Plan** and had a remaining balance to be paid, it will be included as an income in the tax return for the year of their death.
- If the deceased was a participant of a **Lifelong Learning Plan** and had a remaining balance to be paid, it could be included as an income in the tax return for the year of their death. There is also the option for the surviving spouse to continue to make the repayments. (you should consult your accountant for this choice)
- If the spouse is named beneficiary of the RRSP or RIF it will be rolled over to them with no tax implications. When the spouse starts receiving RIF payments, it will be included in their yearly income.
- If the RRSP/RIF beneficiary is not a spouse, the Fair Market Value of the account is included in the deceased annuitant's income for the year of death.
- Rule of thumb: the day that you die is the day that you are considered to have sold all of your assets.
- Discuss this with your advisor.

Be aware of RRSP scams.

Some people were approached with this scam. If Revenue Canada mentions this on their website, it is because it is pretty common.

- The scheme offers amazing returns that sound too good to be true.
- It sometimes offers 'guaranteed' monthly payments.
- They tell you to withdraw your RRSP, and pay no attention to the income taxes withheld, you will be getting them back from them.
- They promise income tax receipts that will provide deductions of three or more times the amount contributed to a RRSP.
- The reason why these scams work , it is because the first people to get hooked do really get high monthly payments, and then they tell their friends. Once they discover it is a scam, their money is gone.
- Protect yourself by checking into their professional licences.
- Google the person's name to see if any previous penalties or fraud charges come up.

LIRA: Locked-in retirement account

A LIRA is simply :

- If you have a **pension plan** through your employer and you leave your job, you'll have to decide what to do with your pension. One of your options may be to transfer it into a LIRA.
- It is locked-in, meaning you cannot withdraw until you reach a certain age.
- Since the account comes from a pension plan, you cannot contribute to it.

TFSA

The TFSA came out in 2009 with a $5000 contribution room and we knew this will be quite interesting. These are the details of a TFSA:

- It stands for Tax-free savings account.
- Everyone has the same yearly contribution room.
- You have the contribution room starting the year that you turn 18.
- It is a type of account, not an investment. Do not ask 'which TFSA has the best performance'. An account does not have performance, investments do.
- What you can hold inside the TFSA depends entirely on where your TFSA is. (just like the RRSP)
- You can withdraw as much as you'd like.
- You can deposit the maximum every year, plus any withdrawals you did last year.

- It is really tax-free. No income taxes paid on growth of the account, nor at the moment of withdrawal.
- It does **not** give you a tax deduction.
- The contribution room is carried forward. You can open a TFSA in 2025 and contribute all the way back to 2009. (if you were 18 in 2009)

FHSA

- First home savings account
- You must be 18 and less than 71 and a Canadian Resident.
- It started in 2023, and you do not have the 2023 unless you opened it in 2023. You lose the yearly room for the years it was not opened, unlike the TFSA.
- Rules are similar to the HBP: you do not currently live in a qualifying home, in this calendar year or the previous 4.
- It seems like there will be a question on the income tax return inquiring if you opened a FHSA in 2023. At the time I am writing this, the government website is not up to date.
- Contribution room is $8000 per year, and a lifetime amount of$40K.
- Similar to other types of accounts, you can open more than one, but do not go over your room.
- You cannot contribute in another person's FHSA.
- The contributions give you a tax-deduction.
- There is a maximum participation period: the 15th anniversary of opening your first FHSA and/ or the year you turn 71. So this means, you have 15 years to buy a home using the FHSA.
- Before the end of your plan, you can transfer to a RRSP.

IPP

If you are an entrepreneur, this information is important to know.

- This is a defined benefit pension plan for one person.
- The IPP is ideal for the entrepreneur who is between 45 and 65.
- The corporation makes the contributions to your plan and gets a tax-deduction for it.
- The corporation can also deduct interest on borrowed funds, actuarial fees, accounting fees, and even investment advising fees paid.
- Provides a guaranteed retirement income.
- The IPP has a greater contribution limit than the RRSP.
- Ideal for business owners who pay themselves a salary, of at least $120K, and have maximised their RRSP.
- IPP assets are generally safe from creditors.
- Since it is a defined-benefit plan, the corporation can top-up contributions if investment returns were not high enough to fund the promised benefit to you.
- The corporation can also make a lump-sum contribution for past-services.
- Income from IPP are eligible for income splitting with you spouse.

- The disadvantages of an IPP
  - there are costs to set up and ongoing yearly actuarial fees.
  - There are withdrawal restrictions, the funds are locked-in until retirement.
  - No spousal contributions allowed.

RRIF:

Information given above in the RRSP section. A RRIF comes from the RRSP that has matured.

LIF

A LIF is similar to a RIF in every way, except it has a maximum yearly amount, meaning you cannot withdraw more than what the government allows.

RESP

The next chapter is all about RESP's.

RDSP

Registered Disability savings Plan

- A savings plan to help an individual who is approved to receive the DTC, disability tax credit, to save for their long-term financial security.
- Contributions are not tax deductible and can be made until the beneficiary turns 59.
- When withdrawing from the plan , your capital, (contributions) are not included as income to the beneficiary, but the grant, the bond and investment income are.
- You can only have ONE plan at any given time.
- Anyone can contribute to a RDSP, with the permission of the account holder.
- No annual contribution limit, but a lifetime of $200,000
- Your RRSP can be rolled over at death to your financially dependant child or grandchild, to their RDSP. The maximum roll-over is $200K.
- If the RDSP receives a roll-over from a RRSP, that amount is not eligible for the grant.
- New contributions are not allowed if the beneficiary is no longer approved for DTC.
- amounts from a deceased parent or grandparent's RRSP, RRIF, RPP, PRPP or SPP which the beneficiary was financially dependent for support, can be rolled over into the RDSP provided the rollover is completed before the end of the fifth taxation year throughout which the beneficiary is no longer DTC-eligible

- The RDSP **must** be closed and all amounts remaining in the plan must be paid out to the beneficiary's estate by December 31st of the year **following** the calendar year in which the beneficiary dies.
- A DAP is any payment from an RDSP to the beneficiary or to their estate after their death.
- LDAPs are disability assistance payments (DAPs) that, once started, must be paid at least annually until either the plan is terminated or the beneficiary has died.

The RDSP is the type of account that is the least understood, and not every financial institution can open them.

This is a great tool if you have a child for whom you receive the DTC and are worried about the financial future. Just like any other type of account, discuss this with an advisor.

Chapter Ten
Regular RESP vs Group RESP.

I was about 12 when I found out about RESP's, I guess from school. I thought I understood the plan, but then a guy from a **Group RESP plan**, let's pretend from Universitas, knocked at my house and I was standing next to my mom while the guy was explaining. This was many years ago, but this is what I remember the guy saying, trying to convince my mom to join:

- You contribute, and your money is pooled with other parents' money.
- When your daughter does to post-secondary school, like Cegep or University, she receives payments from the plan.
- The great news is, if for her age-group, she is part of a small group of students who go to school, she will be getting money that were contributed from other parents.

My thoughts?

- This is evil, you are benefitting from other people's hard-earned money that they contributed for their OWN kid.
- You will be hoping that a lot of students do not pursue post-secondary education.
- You are wishing for a parent's worst-nightmare, that their kid becomes a drop-out.

At that time, I remember looking at my mom with a look of 'WTF is this".

Since then, I have always hated those plans, and do not understand why there are not more lawsuits, and how the government allows this.

If you Google those plans, you will see plenty of complaints. Over the years, there have been plenty of articles about this plan, including from CBC and Global News. The complaints are mostly about the fees and the difficulty of withdrawing funds.

In 2021 , Quebec has authorized a class-action lawsuit against Group RESP's. (this is from the Global News website)

Quebec **class-action lawsuit** against providers of group registered educations savings plans (**group RESPs**) could have ripple effects across Canada.

The lawsuit, which was authorized by the **Superior Court of Quebec** on March 31, targets six group RESP providers alleging that the sales charges or enrolment fees they have been charging in Quebec are unlawful and, in some cases, abusive. Authorization of a class-action lawsuit in Quebec is similar to a certification of a class-action lawsuit in other provinces.

Specifically, the lawsuit is targeting Canadians C.S.T. Consultants Inc. and Canadian Scholarship Trust Foundation; Kaleido Growth (previously Universitas Management) and Kaleido Foundation (Previously Universitas Foundation Of Canada); Knowledge First Financial (previously Heritage Education Funds Inc.) and Knowledge First Foundation; Heritage Education Funds and Heritage Educational Foundation; Children's Education Funds Inc. and Children's Educational Foundation Of Canada; and Global RESP Corporation along with Global Educational Trust Foundation.

I will be completely unprofessional right now and will not disclose the "advantages' of a RESP, because as far as I am concerned, it is the type of account to stay away from.

Open a good old regular RESP from your bank or other financial institution that you trust.

If you DO have a Group RESP and would like to know what EXACTLY you have gotten into, let's read the 100-page disclaimers and make sure you understand.

Regular RESP, (with a regular financial institution)

- Registered Education Savings Plan
- Save for your child's education after high school: trade schools, Cegep, colleges, universities, and apprenticeship programs.
- Adults can also open one for themselves.
- The financial institution will apply for the Canada Learning Bond and the Canada Education Savings Grant. BC and Quebec also offer provincial benefits.
- These are some basic details, you should view the government website for complete information.

How a RESP works:

- **Canada Learning Bond (CLB)** : has a lifetime maximum, up to $2000 for families with *low income.*
    - No contributions to the RESP are needed to get the CLB
    - The beneficiary could receive $500 the first year they're eligible, then another $100 each eligible year after that until the age of 15
    - The CLB is retroactive. The beneficiary can still be eligible to receive it up to the day before they turn 21.
    - Check the government website for the family income maximums. For example, families with 1 to 3 children will receive the CLB if the family income is less than $53,359.
    - The beneficiary must:
        - be a resident of Canada.
        - have a Social Insurance Number (SIN)
        - be named as a beneficiary in an RESP.
        - be born on or after January 1, 2004
    - The primary caregiver must:
        - Have filed income tax returns for each year they wish to request the CLB for.
        - Be eligible to receive the Canada Child Benefit
    - Children in care, for whom a Children's Special allowance is payable, are also eligible.
    - Adults born in 2004 or later may receive the Learning Bond for themselves until the age of 21.

British Colombia Training and Education Savings grant (BCTESG).

- The B.C. Government will contribute $1,200 to eligible children through the BCTESG. Children may apply for the grant between their 6th birthday and the day before they turn 9.
- The parent or guardian plus the child must be residents of British Columbia at the time of application and have a valid Social Insurance Number.

Quebec Education Savings Incentive (QESI)

- has a lifetime maximum of $3600.
- You need to make a contribution to get the grant.
- You get 10% of your yearly contributions.

- **Canada Education Savings Grant**: has a lifetime maximum of $7200.
    - ○ Contributions must be made to the RESP to get the CESG.
    - ○ The CESG can add a maximum of $500 to a RESP each year, and up to another $100 for eligible families with middle- and low-income
    - ○ Receive up to 20% grant of the first $2500 per year.
    - ○ If you do not receive the maximum CESG amount in a given year, you can still receive it in future years. You can catch up on this amount by making more contributions to the RESP.
    - ○ You can catch up one year at a time.
    - ○ The CESG is available until the end of the calendar year that the beneficiary turns 17
    - ○ The beneficiary:
        - ▪ Must be a resident of Canada
        - ▪ have a Social Insurance Number (SIN)
        - ▪ be named as a beneficiary in an RESP
    - ○ Once your child reaches 16 or 17 , they must be eligible to get the CESG. They must meet at least one criterion:
        - ▪ A total of at least $2000 has been contributed and not withdrawn.
        - ▪ A minimum annual contribution of $100 and not withdrawn in the past four years.
    - ○ There is no annual limit as to how much you can contribute. $2500 is to reach the maximum yearly grant, but you can deposit more if you wish.
    - ○ The lifetime contribution limit is $50,000 per child
    - ○ Contributions above the $50K per child has a penalty of 1% per month.

Opening an account:

- You can open an individual plan or a family plan.
- You can open more than one account, but the total contributions must not exceed the maximums. If there are 2 parents who unknowingly both open an account, it will be the first one who contributed who will get the grants. (for example, if you contribute $2500 in January, and your ex-spouse contributes $2500 in March, you will get the grant).
- Any adult can open a RESP account for a child- parents, guardians, grandparents, other relatives, and friends. (If someone other than the parents open the RESP, the RESP might be part of the person's estate if they die. We are beginning to see complications with RESP that has a grandparent subscriber) Have a discussion with your advisor.
- The financial institution needs a name, DOB and SIN to open the account.
- Not every financial institution offers all grants. If you are in Quebec, there are some promoters who do not offer the QESI. So, ask before opening the account.
- Check if the financial institution:
  - offers both single and family plans.
  - Have fees.
  - Do they have minimums, for example $25 per transaction?
  - What will it be invested in?
- The subscriber is the person who opens the RESP.
- You and your spouse can be joint subscribers, but beware that at the time of withdrawal, you will need both signatures.

- The beneficiary is the person who will get the money to pay for their education. (In this case, a beneficiary does not mean who gets the account if the owner dies)
- A single plan is for one beneficiary
- A family plan can have more than one beneficiary.
- The financial institution who is opening the account for you is called the promoter.

Individual (non-family) plan :

- An option if you only have one child, or if you are not related to the child you are saving for.
- In this plan, there is only one beneficiary allowed.

Family plan: We often open a Family Plan for our clients, even when they have only one child, because you never know the future. Adding a beneficiary is simply done with a form, and as long as it follows the rules:
- the child must be related to you by blood or adoption, and they must:
- be under 21 years old at the time you add them to the plan; or have been a beneficiary of another family RESP immediately before being added to this one
- If you add a beneficiary who is not a sibling already named on the plan, you will need to repay the benefits to the government.
- Nieces, nephews, aunts, uncles and cousins are not considered blood relatives.
- The advantage of a family plan is that earnings can be shared among the children, and the CESG may be used by any eligible beneficiary named in the RESP, to a maximum of $7,200 per child.
- The QESI can be shared among the beneficiaries.

Withdrawals:

Many years ago, we used to ask for receipts for every withdrawal. Now, we will ask for proof of expenses if you are requesting to withdraw more than what the plan allows. Keep all of your receipts, the government can audit any withdrawal, regardless of the amount withdrawn.

A RESP can be used to pay tuition, books, tools, transportation, and rent.

When it is time to withdraw, your financial institution must follow the rules, and you could get penalties if you go against these.

A RESP accumulates over time:
- Contributions you have made (your capital)
- Benefits, the grants and bond.
- Interest accumulated (or growth)

At the time of withdrawal, the financial institution will ask you what type of withdrawal you are making and might require a form and proof of education (if your child is pursuing their post-secondary education). There are 3 ways to withdraw:
- Educational Assistance Payments
- A withdrawal of contributions
- Accumulated Income Payment

Educational Assistance Payments;

- An amount paid to help finance the cost of post-secondary education.
    - the student is enrolled in a qualifying educational program. This includes students attending a post-secondary educational institution and those enrolled in distance education courses, such as correspondence courses, provided by such institutions
    - the student has attained the age of 16 years and is enrolled in a specified educational program
- It can be paid to the subscriber or to the beneficiary.
- Taxed in the hands of the beneficiary, they will receive a T4A slip.
- A beneficiary must be a resident of Canada to receive the CESG or CLB as part of the EAP.
- The beneficiary can receive EAP's up to six months after ceasing enrollment.
- A qualifying program: post-secondary level that lasts at least three weeks and requires the student to spend at least 10 hours per week. The list of certified institutions can be found online.
- A specified educational program at post-secondary level that lasts at least three weeks and the student spends at least 12 hours per month.
- The EAP amounts are : EAP limits have now increased from $5,000 to $8,000 in the first 13 weeks of enrollment in a qualifying educational program (full-time studies), and from $2,500 to $4,000

in any 13-week period while enrolled in a specified educational program (part-time studies) as of March 28, 2023

- In 2024, the annual EAP limit is $28,122.
- If you require a higher EAP, you may contact the CESA, Canada Education Savings Act. They might approve on a case-by-case basis. 1-888-276-3624.

A withdrawal of contributions

- If your child does not go to post-secondary education, your contributions can be returned tax-free.
- The payment can be made to the subscriber or to the beneficiary.
- This type of withdrawal should only be made if you are sure will not go back to school, since there are consequences :
  - o If you ever need to withdraw some of your original contributions for non-educational purposes and there is no beneficiary of the plan who is currently eligible to receive an EAP, any CESG that you received for the original contributions will need to be repaid to the federal government.
- In a family plan :
  - o If the CESG-assisted contributions are withdrawn after March 22, 2004, all beneficiaries under the RESP are ineligible for the Additional CESG in the year of withdrawal and the next two calendar years.
  - o If contributions made prior to 1998 are withdrawn, all beneficiaries under the RESP are not eligible to receive the CESG in that year and for the next two calendar years.
  - o Since these rules are subject to change, you should check the government website for any changes.

Accumulated Income Payment

- Accumulated income payment (AIPs) are amounts, usually paid to the subscriber, of the income earned from an RESP.
- When your child is not pursuing post-secondary education.
- Also, any one of the following three conditions must also apply
    - the payment is made after the year that includes the 9th anniversary of the RESP and each individual (other than a deceased individual) who is or was a beneficiary has **reached 21 years of age** and is not currently eligible to receive an EAP (see "Note" below)
    - the payment is made in the year that includes the **35th anniversary of the RESP,** unless the RESP is a specified plan in which case the payment is made in the year that includes the 40th anniversary of the RESP
    - all the beneficiaries under the RESP are **deceased** when the payment is made
    - We may waive the conditions in the first bullet if it is reasonable to expect that a beneficiary under the RESP will not be able to pursue post-secondary education because they suffer from a severe and prolonged mental impairment. Such requests have to be made by the RESP promoter in writing to the following address:

        Canada Revenue Agency
        Registered Plans Directorate
        875 Heron Rd.
        Ottawa ON K1A 0L5

- An RESP must be terminated by the end of February of the year after the year in which the first AIP is paid.
- An AIP is subject to two different taxes: the regular income tax and an additional tax of 20% (12% for residents of Quebec). (see website for details)

Keeping track: Your advisor can keep track if you open the account with them and stay with them. It is a little bit harder to do when accounts are transferred from one place to another.

Transfers : regular RESP plans (not group plans) allow you to transfer your account to another institution of your choosing.

Rolling over to RDSP. To qualify for an education savings rollover, the beneficiary must meet the existing age and residency requirements in relation to RDSP contributions. As well, one of the following conditions must be met:

- the beneficiary is, or will be, unable to pursue post-secondary education because they have a severe and prolonged mental impairment
- the RESP has been in existence for at least 35 years
- the RESP has been in existence for at least 10 years and each beneficiary under the RESP has attained 21 years of age and is not eligible to receive educational assistance payments
- You need consent from the RDSP holder.

When you are unsure of your contributions and grants of your plan, you should contact the government: Toll-free in Canada and the United States: 1-800-267-3100.

Chapter 11
Your Pension

In Canada, we are lucky to have access to a pension when we retire.

When making a retirement plan, your advisor will ask you for your pension statement. The statement shows how much QPP or CPP you will receive .

The Canada Pension Plan, CPP:

- o monthly, taxable benefit that replaces part of your income when you retire. If you qualify, you'll receive the CPP retirement pension for the rest of your life.
- o Everyone's amount is different.
- o Eligibility for CPP is determined by your contributions to the plan and your age.
- o To qualify, you must be at least 60 years of age and have made at least one valid contribution to the plan.
- o You can receive the CPP and still continue to work.
- o Income does not reduce the CPP you receive, it actually increases if you continue paying into it until age of 70.
- o Once you reach 65, you can stop paying into the CPP.
- o Once you reach 70, the CPP stops, even if you are still working.
- o You can start receiving it at 60, and as late as 70.
- o Most advisors will recommend waiting as long as possible to take it.
- o If you start receiving it at 60, the amount you will receive, until you die, will be smaller than if you would have waited until 70. For those of you with a life expectancy in your 90's, it is important to consider.

Your age affects your pension amount:

- If you start before age 65, payments will decrease by 0.6% each month (or by 7.2% per year), up to a maximum reduction of 36% if you start at age 60
- If you start after age 65, payments will increase by 0.7% each month (or by 8.4% per year), up to a maximum increase of 42% if you start at age 70 (or after).

How much you will receive will depend on a few things :

- the age you decide to start your pension
- how much and for how long you contributed to the CPP
- your average earnings throughout your working life
- You might have years of low or no earnings. The CPP will "drop out" or not include up to 8 years of your lowest earnings from your earnings history. This will increase the amount of your pension.
- For 2024, the maximum monthly amount you could receive if you start your pension at age 65 is $1,364.60. You can get an estimate through the government website, and you should receive an annual statement.
- If you have received a CPP disability pension:
    - The CPP will "drop out" or not include those months when calculating the base component of your CPP benefit.
    - but will "drop in" credits for the time you were disabled

Pension sharing is allowed with your spouse or common-law partner.

Separation or divorce: The CPP contributions can be split equally between you and your spouse/common-law partner.

The CPP survivor's pension is a monthly payment paid to the legal spouse or common-law partner of the deceased contributor, and the amount you receive will depend on:

- o   whether you are younger or older than age 65
- o   how much, and for how long, the deceased contributor has paid into the CPP

The Quebec Pension Plan, QPP

- o If you live in Quebec, you do not participate in the CPP, but the QPP.
- o It is a compulsory public insurance plan
    - o Financial protection at retirement, death and disability.
- o Contributors are 18 and over and have a yearly income of more than $3500
- o Since 2019 there has been an increase in the contribution rate.
- o The employee and the employer each pay half the contribution to the Québec Pension Plan.
- o Self-employed workers pay the entire contribution.
- o n 2024, the contribution rate for the QPP is 10.8%
- o That rate is split equally between the employer and the employee,
- o and applies to part of the employment earnings between the $3500 general exemption and $68 500, which is the maximum amount on which employees can contribute in 2024.
- o Similar to the CPP, the longer you wait, the higher your pension amount will be:
    - o Age 60:   you wil receive 64% of the max
    - o Age 65: you will receive 100% of the max
    - o Age 70: you will get 142% of the max
- o Same as CPP, the QPP retirement payment they receive is based on how much they have contributed to the plan.
- o More info can be found on RRQ.gouv.qc.ca

Old Age Security, OAS

- o This is from the Canadian Government
- o Most people are enrolled automatically and receive a letter after their 64th birthday.
- o Not based on employment history, you must:
    - o be 65 years old or older.
    - o be a Canadian citizen or a legal resident at the time we approve your OAS pension application.
    - o have resided in Canada for at least 10 years since the age of 18
    - o If you are living outside Canada, you must:
        - be 65 years old or older
        - have been a Canadian citizen or a legal resident of Canada on the day before you left Canada
        - have resided in Canada for at least 20 years since the age of 18
- o Everyone receives the same amount, but there is a clawback if you make over $81,761 (amount quoted as of 2022).
- o If you make less than a certain amount, you will receive the Guaranteed Income Supplement:
        - For example if you are single , over 65 and make less than $21,624.
- o See more information on the government website.

When making a retirement plan, our financial planning tool calculates the OAS for us . When it comes to the CPP and QPP, the software can make an estimate, but it is always better if you give your statement to your advisor.

If you are not in Canada, you must learn about what is offered to you.

Do you have types of accounts that grow tax-free?

Do you have types of accounts for your children's education?

What are the accounts that are rolled tax-free to a spouse or financially dependent child?

What are the tools that you have to save for retirement?

Do you know all of what the government can offer you for benefits and retirement?

Make a list of questions to ask your advisor:

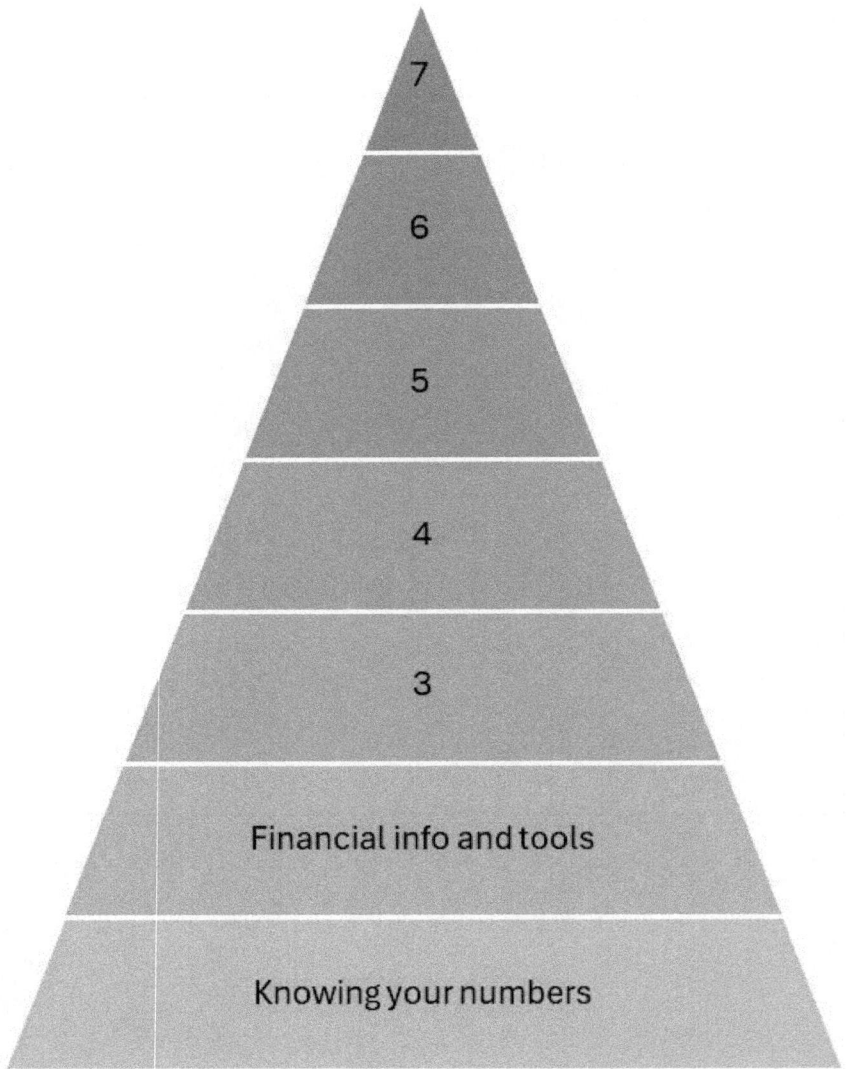

Family life

Chapter Twelve

Protecting your family life

Chapter 12 Glossary---------------------

I have discussed life insurance, critical illness insurance, disability insurance, accident and pet insurance in chapter one. Here are more terms you need to know :

Will, or Last Will and Testament.

- Depending on where you live, you would do this document with a lawyer.
- If you live in Quebec, we recommend doing it with a notary. Note that a lawyer can also create a will, but it will then be a different type: a will "made in front of witnesses".
- Some places recognise a handwritten Will or typed, but be advised, that it might make things complicated for your loved ones. In Quebec, the hand-written Will or a typed one must be probated by the court, which will cause a lot of fees and time.
- In this document, you will name:
    - the person (s) who will act as liquidator (executor)
    - your beneficiaries
    - a guardian for your children if you were to both pass away.
- Keep in mind that in a Will, you cannot remove someone's rights. For example, you cannot say that at your death, your children will go live with your sister, not the father.

The liquidator will have all the burden of settling your estate, so choose wisely. You can decide to include a payment for your liquidator, but it is not necessary. When adding someone as liquidator to your Will, it is a best practice to tell the person beforehand. "sis, you are it".

When naming a guardian for your children, you can name one person who will take care of them physically, and you can also name one person who will oversee the finances. This is especially useful if you do not want your ex to get a hold of your assets.

Mandate

I use the short term, mandate. But you might know it as :

- Mandate in case of capacity
- Mandate of protection
- *Continuing power of Attorney* . Do not confuse this with a general power of attorney. And in Quebec, we do not have this.

You can name someone who will take care of your medical decisions. You can name a different person who will take care of the finances. It is useful if you do not want your kids to only think about money and have the power to unplug you. (kidding, not kidding) . It can be the same person. You can name multiple people.

Power of Attorney

- A power of attorney gives the person **full power**, as of right now, to do EVERYTHING as if they are you. Liquidate accounts, buy real estate, etc .
- You will need to go back to the lawyer or notary to remove it.
- Or it becomes null if you become incapacitated.
- We have all seen Rocky V, if I remember correctly, Rocky lost everything because his accountant had a POA and took everything.
- It is useful between spouses, or you can grant it to one of your children. It is especially useful when one spouse is in the army and is often away.
- It is not a document that like personally, it gives the person too much power.

A continuing Power of Attorney : this does not exist in Quebec. The POA continues even when the person becomes incapacitated.

A Power of attorney for personal care : this does not exist in Quebec. It covers your personal decisions, such as housing and health care.

Trading Authorisation: you are giving authorisation for someone to do things with your accounts, but not giving them ALL the power.

- The person can buy or sell your investments,
- Make investment decisions.
- Tell your advisor to send you money.
- But cannot withdraw money to send to themselves.
- This is useful when you hate talking to your advisor about your investments and want your spouse to take care of it. The advisor might naturally talk to one spouse more than the other, but the document should be in place to make things official.

Trusted contact: there might be other names for it. It is a name and contact information of a person you trust , that you give to your financial advisor. They are to contact the person only if:

- They think you are starting to loose your marbles.
- They think you might be getting scammed and are worried
- They cannot get a hold of you.
- It is not meant to be an authorization to solicit this person.

Shareholder agreement:

This is the most important document to do if you have a business with a partner. NO MATTER WHO THE PARTNER IS. The document will have clauses about:

- Who inherits your part of the business if you die? You do NOT want to have to share the business with a partner you did not choose. You can imagine the stories I have.
- What is done if you become sick, for more than a period, and cannot perform your duties?
  - Does the other partner become full owner?
  - Do they have to hire someone until you pass away?
  - Do they have to pay your beneficiaries the fair market value of your share?
- What happens if one of you wants out?
- What happens if one of you causes irreparable distress to the business' reputation?
- What happens if one of you causes any type of harm to the business' finances?
- What happens if any one you gets a criminal record, or goes to jail ?
- Are you 50-50 ? or 51-49 ?
- Did one person put up their own money and would want their investment back ?
- Who keeps the business if there is to be a split ? Will the aseets be divided, or only the shares ?

-------------end of Glossary--------------------------------

Why do financial advisors always want to discuss Wills, Mandates, Power of Attorney, Trusted Contact, insurance, and disability?

Because, we have seen that there are worst things for your finances that a market crash. When we meet with someone, and the first thing they say is "I have a little bit of savings, and I want to make sure that I do well with it".... Ok, let's start at the beginning, at the bottom of the pyramid.

I cannot answer what to do with your $30K savings unless I know where you are. How safe is your family?

Single :

Myth : **"I am single and have no kids, so I don't need any type of insurance or a Will."**   Wrong for so many reasons.

I would ask you :

- If you get sick, and this would keep you out of work for 2 years, would you be able to survive financially?
- You might answer : " I have coverage at work".
    - What type of long-term coverage? It is always a percentage, let's say 50% of your income, and $1500 max per month.
    - With these numbers, could you survive financially?
- And if you get sick, do you know that no one can legally go into your account and pay your bills for you, if you do not have a mandate?
- What if you are in a coma, and you did not put a mandate in place, you trust that whoever the court appoints will make the best decision for you ? Financially ? Medically ?
- If you are to pass away, and the law states that your assets go to your siblings, are you ok with that?
- If you are to pass away before your parents, do you think your parents can go back to work after 4 days? (often at work, we get 4 days off when someone passes away).
- Even if you are single and have no kids, you are leaving such a burden to your loved ones to get things done if you are sick, in a coma or pass away.

Common-law spouse

If you are common-law, you are not as protected as you think.

Death : Depending on where you live and its civil code, a lot of times common-law spouses do not inherit anything if the spouse passes away. If there are kids, the kids inherit everything. If there are no kids, it goes to the parents and or siblings.

Separation : In the case of a separation, there is no family patrimony, no assets need to be divided.

- I heard a woman say " I gave him $1000 per month to help pay for mortgage and utilities, so half the house is mine". Not true, if your name is not on the house, you are not an owner.
- A man once told his ex-girlfriend that she owed him all the money he spent on her. Not true.
- If there are children involved, they have the same rights, no matter if the parents were married or not.
- Dividing up furniture and other assets simply means you need to determine who owns it, legally. If there are 2 cars, both in his name, but you were driving one car, too bad they are both in is name.

Illness or disability :

Let's say you make most of the money and take care of finances. You get really sick and are in a coma. Your spouse is not legally allowed to go into your bank account and pay bills for you. Without a mandate, married or not, no one is able to take care of your finances for you.

If you have cancer, and you have disability insurance from work, great, but your spouse will not be able to take time off work to help you with your medical appointments, unless they have a "compassionate' insurance through their work, or unless you have a Critical Illness Insurance to cover their missed salary. (as mentioned above, Disability coverage pays for your salary. Often in a couple, both salaries are important to survive financially) .

Other family members. What if you have your financial *shit* together, (for lack of a better term) , but someone close to you does not. Something happens, will you help them out financially? There are plenty of people who get in trouble financially because they helped someone else out. It is time that siblings talk to each other about he 'what-ifs".

And maybe you will need to refuse to help if it will burden you financially to the point of bankruptcy.

I wish siblings would talk openly about this stuff :

- What if something happens to mom or dad, do they have a mandate, a Power of attorney, a Will , insurance , long-term care insurance ?
- How do you see the division of the physical help they will need?
- And financially ?
- Do all of *you, siblings,* have their legal documents in order?
- If you have a great financial advisor, who helped you put all of this in place, maybe it is time to introduce them to your siblings, (if they openly tell you that they do not have all of this in place).

If you are married, and have no Will:

It is a myth that if you are married, you are protected 100%.

Depending on where you live, if your spouse were to pass away, without a Will, you will only get 1/3, and the children 2/3, for example.

- Since we are living in a time where there are plenty of blended families, make sure you understand: 2/3 to ALL of their children. If your spouse has 4 children with another woman, and one with you, ALL 5 children get 2/3 of the assets.
- Legislation of where you live will determine who receives what :
  - Your home
  - Your business
  - Bank accounts
  - Family heirlooms
  - Investments and savings
  - Even joint accounts. For example, in Quebec, there is no rights of survivorship. Meaning, if your spouse passes away, the joint account does not become 100% yours.
- Business. Imagine your spouse dying, and instead of inheriting 100% of the business, you must now share it with the spouse's only child? The child becomes your business partner.

Business

A woman once reached out to me and asked me about "how to invest to make the most money", but I asked her the same questions as I always do, but found this out, she has:

- A blended family, and a child with a severe disability.
- A business that she owns 100%
- A business that she owns with someone else.
- A house that she owns with her spouse.
- Real estate that she owns with her father
- Real estate that she owns with 2 other friends

You can guess, I did not care about how she wants to invest before I knew exactly where she was at with the base of her pyramid. My questions were :

- Do you have a RDSP for the severely handicapped child?
- Do you have a Will, and a mandate?
- Do you have a shareholder agreement for the businesses and real estate you own with others?
- Does your father have a Will , and does the real estate you hold with him go back to you 100% ?
- Do you have life , DI and CI insurance ?
- Do you have any pets ?
- Do you have an emergency fund ?
- Do you have RESP's for the other children?
- What type of protection does your spouse have ?

It is probably frustrating for someone who wants to discuss investments, and my first words are "nope, not going there until we discuss your biggest risks ". Or I tell them : " ok, we will open the accounts, and have the investment discussion, but we WILL make the time to put all the other things in place."

We have the discussion because we are freaking out at ALL the things that could go wrong, and I am not even thinking about a market crash.

We are able to analyse situations pretty quickly and know exactly where your risks are. I hope you have an advisor that does this for you.

Putting things in place to reduce your biggest risks is more important than discussing the latest ETF or Crypto.

Chapter Thirteen
Facing reality about expenses.

What is probably the biggest cause for divorces?

Money
The lack of it.
The frustration around it.
The lack of communication.
The unrealistic view on what things cost.

You can guess, I do have plenty of stories. Since 2018, when I got my first divorce designation, CDFA, Certified Divorce Financial Specialist, I had plenty of discussions with people going through a divorce.

The reason why this chapter is about facing the reality about expenses, is because I often noticed that one spouse had no clue how expensive everything is.

Here is a story: the story is changed a little, I would not want to give too much personal info on someone.

A woman once was very sure that her husband was hiding money, because, as she said, 'he makes a ton of money, and he says we are struggling financially and is asking me to start working".
It is possible that someone is hiding money, but here are details as she saw them:

- The husband makes $125K as a director
- She does not work, never did, because he promised her that she would never have to work.
- They have a house with a mortgage of $2500. They have a car each, and the monthly payments come to $1800.
- She asked me how much I think her husband is hiding.
- You can guess my answer: he is not hiding money from you but is probably hiding a lot of debt from you.
- She was surprised by my answer, I guess she did not do the math:
  - In Quebec, a gross salary of $125K is $87K net, which is $7250 per month.
  - Their mortgage, taxes, hydro, car payments and gas came to $5620.
  - We did not even calculate daycare (yes, even though she did not work, she sent her kids to daycare) .
  - We did not calculate yet groceries, wifi, cells, cable, snow removal contract, and summer camps, clothing, birthday gifts, insurances, gym membership, private clinic membership, car repairs, restaurants, Starbucks, her nails and hair.
  - I asked her what she did for the kids' birthdays, she told me that the last birthday was done in a movie theater, and they had invited 20 friends. She spent about $700 on the cake, food, snacks, loot bags and movie.

- My guess was that he was at least $50K in debt, and I was right, he was at $75K credit card and line of credit. (maybe more, but he was too embarrassed to tell me).

When he asked her to start working to help pay the bills, she started the process of a divorce, and she still insisted that with $125K per year, he will be able to pay her to stay home.

In this case, even when showing her the monthly expenses versus income, she still did not believe it.

Here is another story:

Together they make $130,000 gross.
He makes $3500 net per month.
She makes $4000 net per month.

She was telling me that with this salary, ***they feel like they should be able to afford*** a house, 2 cars, family trips, and be able to give to their church.

They used to be in an apartment that was $1000 per month, but they felt like they deserved better, and wanted to show their families that they were successful, so they had moved into an apartment that is currently $1800 per month. (no judgement, but the best decision would have been to stay put and save for a house)

They feel like that would be able to afford a mortgage of around $3500. Just from this, ***I hope you are saying "NOPE", the math is not mathing.*** (if you are not, I am guessing you skipped the chapter about budget and the 50-30-20 rule)

Just from that statement, I knew they never did the math. A lot of people with salary ranges between $100K to $150K have a completely skewed version of today's cost of living. (dude, you are stuck in the 80's) .

A mortgage of $3500 is using **47%** of their monthly income.

As mentioned, housing, transportation and groceries **should be at 50%,** this is their numbers, calculated monthly: (they are way over he 50%)

50% for housing, transportation and food	
Rent	3 500,00 $
Hydro	150,00 $
Car Payment	398,00 $
Car & Tenant Insurance	225,00 $
OPUS card	155,00 $
Fuel (car)	500,00 $
Food - Groceries	1 500,00 $
Food - Eating Out/Ordering In	150,00 $
Car Registration	22,50 $
Oil Changes	60,00 $
Driver Licences	14,17 $
	6 674,67 $
ratio	89%

So, **with $825.33 left per month**, this is what their dollars were supposed to spread enough for:

30% is for the rest	
2 Cells	156,00 $
Internet and Wifi	58,00 $
Bank Fees for 2 chequing accounts	30,00 $
School Daycare	400,00 $
Birthdays/Gifts/ Xmas	80,00 $
icloud storage	2,00 $
Amazon Prime	9,50 $
Optometrist	30,00 $
Haircuts	60,00 $
Medical, private clinic	30,00 $
Costco Membership	5,00 $
Epipens	10,00 $
School fees	30,00 $
Dental	40,00 $
Prescriptions	40,00 $
Summer camps	50,00 $
Winter snow removal	20,00 $
Life insurance for both	120,00 $
Critical Illness insurance for her only	60,00 $
Accounting fees	30,00 $
School pictures	10,00 $
CAA Quebec membership	12,00 $
Clothing and shoes for 4 people	200,00 $
house small renovations and repairs	100,00 $
March break and summer vacation	200,00 $
School fundraising	10,00 $
Back-to -school supplies	20,00 $
occasional SAAQ	10,00 $
total	1 822,50 $

The example above is something that we often see. The mortgage payment is too high. They should not have a housing cost that is at 47% of their income.

With these numbers, this couple will be at $50K of debt within a few years.

Both people in the relationship must have a realistic view on how far the dollar can stretch. In this case, it felt like they were both so proud of their income & careers, that they thought they should be able to afford much more than they can.

Chapter Fourteen
The Real Estate
dilemma

This chapter is about answering the two main questions about real estate; should you REALLY buy a house? Is a real estate investment good for me?

Unfortunately, a lot of people feel the pressure to buy a house. It is a societal issue for some, and for others it is a cultural thing. They arrive in Canada and feel the pressure to become rich. They also have the pressure to send money back home. I am not going to go into details of how immigrants struggle when the get here, and face the reality of the American Dream, that is a whole other book that I am not willing to write. I was married to a man who tried all his life to appear rich because he had so much pressure from back home 'to make it'.

Buying a home does not make sense for a lot of people. It is perfectly ok to stay in a rental, as long as you do not move every few years, then, you are chasing the rent increases.

You should not buy a house, if:
- You are in a rental right now and are NOT saving at least 20% of your income.
- You do not know your numbers. Knowing how much you make and your monthly expenses is the first step before even thinking of buying a house.
- You have debt and are not in control of it.
- You don't have a steady job.
- You do not have any type of savings, at least the 5-10% cash down.
- The family income is at least $100K. (for a house of $400K, with a mortgage rate of 6.79% and a monthly payment of $2550).
- If you are single and make less than $65K, you should not even consider it.

Before buying a house:

- At least 6 months before buying a home, calculate how much money you would spend on a mortgage and taxes. LESS what you are currently paying as a rent and SAVE that for at least 6 months. If it is impossible for you, then you should not go ahead.
- Know how much housing costs you can afford per month (mortgage payment plus taxes), using the 50-30-20 rule,
- Do not ignore the 50% rule with the argument that the house will increase in value.
- Save for a down payment. If the house is worth less than $500K, the requirement is 5%. If it is worth more than that, the requirement is 10%.
- Get a pre-approval from the bank.

Pre-approval from the bank:

- The bank will check your credit score and history.
- The bank will ask for proof of income, savings, and investments.
- If a parent is giving you money, they will ask for proof , or a letter from them.
- They will look at your ratios. So do NOT buy an expensive car just before, or do any other type of payment plans.
- **And very important, whatever number the bank comes up with; do NOT buy a house with the maximum of the pre-approval. Let's say you are approved for a house of $600K, you should go for a $450K home.**

Credit scores :

- The minimum credit score needed to buy a house is at least 680.
- Your credit score is affected by:
    - your payment history, if you pay your bills on time.
    - The ratio of credit usage. You should use only 25%
    - Length of credit history. It is important to show a history of good credit behavior. Some people keep credit cards for 30 years, and barely use it.
    - New credit. Credit applications affect your credit score.
    - Types of credit. You need diversity to show good credit behavior, like a line of credit or a car loan.

If you are an entrepreneur:

Nearly 20% of all Canadians are entrepreneurs. It is sometimes hard to get a mortgage, because:

- Income is hard to prove.
- You do not declare all of your income (tax evasion is punishable by jail time, and you can be fined up to 200% of what you really owed)
- You expense so much to pay as little taxes as possible. You NET income is often too small to qualify.

Pre-approval for entrepreneurs.

Of course, the pre-approval process is much easier if you have a lot of savings and investments.

If you have solid proofs of income, and a good cash down, you should be able to get the same mortgage product and rate as a salaried individual. If you have trouble proving income, or your NET seems a little too low compared to your gross, the bank might still approve you, but will require 10% cash down, instead of 5%.

The bank will ask you to provide documents to prove your income:

- Personal and business *Notice of assessments* for 2-3 years
- Financial statements for your business.
- Proof that your HST and/or GST is paid in full.
- Contracts showing expected revenue for the coming years.
- Your personal and business credit scores.
- Proof that you are a principal owner in the business.
- A copy of your borrower's business or GST licence or Article of Incorporation showing you are licensed.
- Proof that your down payment has not been gifted. Meaning, that they might ask for months of account statements to prove that it is really your money.
- If your income is a little hard to verify, they might ask you for up to 6 months of your chequing account, which shows all your business deposits. (make sure your business and personal accounts are separate).

At least 6 months before getting a pre-approval as an entrepreneur:

- Make sure you have a separate budget for yourself and your business.
- You account and credit cards should be separate.
- Your income taxes are to date for both personal and corporate.
- You cleared up all your Revenue Canada debts.
- You have statements that show cash flow, especially if you have a cash business.
- If your business is incorporated, all of your financial statements are up to date
- Have a discussion with a mortgage broker who work with entrepreneurs regularly.

Creating yourself a budget, and sticking to the 50-30-20 rule is important if you are an entrepreneur. If you have the income and the paperwork to prove it, you should be able to get a mortgage.

Real Estate as an investment.

The best tip I ever heard about getting into real estate as an investment is buying a duplex or triplex instead of buying your first home. Generally, buying a duplex or triplex requires 20% cash down. If you will live in the duplex, it falls to 5%, and if you will live in the triplex the amount falls to 10%.

This allows you to be a homeowner and an investor at the same time.

Real estate as an investment has tax consequences. You must declare the income, and at death or at a sale there will be Capital Gains and Capital Recapture. Contrary to investing in a TFSA, where there are absolutely no tax consequences. (unless you overcontribute). Do not let anyone tell you that owning real estate is the only way to get rich. The TSA has made things very interesting for Canadians.

Declaring Real Estate income.
If you own real estate personally, you will have to complete the Federal form T776 (each property must have its own form) which has the following parts:
- Your identification and address of the property
- Details of co-owners
- Income from your tenants
- Expenses
- Calculation of the Capital Cost Claim.

Rental income
You have to declare income, even if one of your tenants "barters" with you. Income can be in the form of cash, a cheque, in goods and services.

Expenses
Let's pretend you bought a triplex, then you will have:
- Expenses for the 2 appartements that you do not live in
- Expenses that were for the whole building, example the entire roof. You will be able to claim only 66.66% of those.

You can deduct the following expenses: (keeping in min the 66.66% ratio, for example)

- Advertising, like advertising for the space to rent in Kijiji.
- Insurance
- Interest charges on the mortgage
- Bank charges. (easier to do if you have a separate bank account)
- Office expenses
- Professional, legal and accounting fees. This includes credit score verification fees.
- Management fees
- Repairs and maintenanve
- Salaries
- Property taxes
- Travel
- Utilities (the ones you pay)

You cannot deduct the mortgage payment. For a lot of people going into real estate, they think that the rents become added monthly income. Do not forget that it is taxable. Since you cannot deduct the mortgage payment, your will try to expense a lot to reduce taxes payable.

You cannot deduct the total cost of the property for the year you purchased it, but there is the Capital Cost Allowance:

- The capital cost allowance is a deduction you can claim over a period of several years for the cost of a depreciable property, like a building, or a car, and machinery.
- You do NOT have to claim a CCA.
- The government has created classes for the different types of property, and the Capital Cost allowance rate that you can use is based on the different classes. For example:
    - You installed sprinkler systems for the entire building. Ou cannot deduct the FULL amount on your income tax returns. This is a class 1 , which is at 4% per year.
    - Machinery is Class 8 , with a 20%
    - Land is NOT a depreciable property.
    - Buildings belong to classes 1,3,6,31 or 32, depending on a few factors. Class 1 includes most buildings acquired after 1987.
    - This means that you can deduct, let's say, 4% of your total cost of purchase every year as a CCA.

Recaptured capital cost allowance.

A huge disappointment when you sell your investment property is when you do the income tax return and realise that there is a Capital Gain and a recapture of the CCA. Both of those means a LOT less money in your pocket. This also means that when you get the check from the notary, do NOT spend everything, you need to save a good chunk of that to pay taxes.

A recapture of the CCA occurs when the proceeds from the sale of the rental property are more than the total of the **undepreciated capital cost** and the capital cost of anything that was added during the year.

Undepreciated capital cost , or Unclaimed Capital Cost is that 4% that you did not decide to use. So, if you have enough expenses in a year, you do not have to claim the CCA, and it turn, it helps you out at the sale of the building.

Horror story:

I often share my story, to show that owning Real Estate property is not always easy.

As with most people, we thought it would be a good idea to go into Real Estate investment. I was hesitant in a way, because I was already taking care of everything, and I knew that this would be another thing for me to take care of, but I still went with it. Heree are the details:

- We had asked our agent to find us something that is profitable.
- We were refinancing our home, to get a cash down for this.
- She showed us a house, where the basement was converted into a bachelor.
- The tenant of the main part of the home was the current owner and wanted to stay there.
- The tenant at the bottom, in the bachelor, was the mother.
- The two of them had dogs, which I was ok with.
- I had the option to kick them out, as per my agent, but I was not ready to take on the responsibility of looking for 2 new tenants. (because if I kicked one one, the other would have left as well) .
- The tenant , who was also the current owner, was giving me a little bit of an attitude, as if it was my fault that she no longer could afford to pay for the house.
- We went to the notary, and everything was fine at first.
- Within a month, there was a fire. The tenant had plugged her Air Conditioning with a very cheap extension cord, and the cord went up in flames.

- A few months later there was water damage. I had asked a handy man to put in a new bathtub, because the old one was a very old one with water jets which were broken. The handy man put in the new tub, but there was something that he forgot to put. This bathtub was in the main part of the house. The thing that he forgot to put, turns out was a very important thing, and it caused water damage all the way to the bottom tenant. We had to remove the walls, had a guy fix the bathtub upstairs. So many expenses.
- A few months later, the main tenant called to tell me that she could not pay the full rent, she was on disability. Every month that she was not paying, caused me to use credit to pay for the mortgage on that house. (so, I was paying 2 mortgages every month). I gave her plenty of chances and was way too patient.
- Where we live, the tenants have more protection than the owners, it would not have been easy to evict her, because she was paying me a little.
- There was also the whole family (and friends) issue. When you have property, some people make you feel like you are obliged to help family and friends, and that if they are looking for a place to stay, you are obligated to rent to them.
- I once rented to a young adult, whom I knew, and I told him that I could help him out and rent it for $350 per month. I only got one month's rent. After that, there was always an excuse NOT to pay.
- It caused a lot of arguments with my spouse, who I had at the time.
- A few months late, we found out that there was a bee infestation.
- The main tenant finally left, but the one that replaced her kept asking for things. I was not charging at market value for the rent and was surprised that they were asking for so much.

Would I go back into real estate as an investment?

Probably not.

- Maximising the TFSA, and having a steady return, seems to me like such an easy answer to build wealth AND it is tax-free, compared to real estate.
- Having tenants is hard.
  - Some are mean.
  - Some do not care about paying their rent.
  - Some think that ALL kitchen sinks come with a food dispenser, *like in the movies*, and they will put bones down there, no matter how many times you tell them. (true story).
  - They expect the nicest and most expensive things, even when they are NOT paying rent. (and use it as an excuse to NOT pay rent). It is a constant struggle.
  - They do not respect the other neighbors, and you are constantly bombarded with complaints.

Should YOU go into real estate as an investment:

- If your decision to go into it as an investment is because you are struggling monthly, and think it is an easy extra income, do not do it. When your tenants do not pay, it is hard. Evicting them is hard, and it is a *long* process.
- It helps if you are handy. Constantly paying for repairs puts a drain on finances.
- It helps if you have savings to cover if tenants do not pay their rent.
- Look into having a management team. So, you do not deal with tenants, a company does.
- Make sure you have all your *stuff* done, personally, before you go into real estate (and I mean your Will, and mandate. Get life insurance, DI and CI.)
- If you are refinancing your home, to get the cash down, make sure you can afford the new mortgage payment, with or without your monthly rents.

I am not against real estate as an investment, but I often see people putting ALL their money into real estate, and this causes financial issues:

- I heard stories of entrepreneurs who have ALL their money stuck in real estate, (true stories, in my community) who:
  - could not afford an emergency tooth canal treatment.
  - Needed brand new winter tires for their BMW, but asked the garage owner if they could help them out.
  - Had to borrow money from family to buy groceries.
- If you were to pass away, without enough life insurance to cover all the Capital Gains, your beneficiaries will have to sell, maybe even at a loss, to pay government taxes. Since Real Estate is not always easy to sell, you are putting your beneficiaries in a tough financial situation.

My recommendation, if you are serious about owning real estate as an investment, is to have regular investments as well. Building wealth is about not putting everything in one basket, and that is especially true with this.

Owning a condo.

I have been in the financial field for almost 20 years now, and I can tell you that I am not ever buying a condo. (not a recommendation, but a personal choice of mine)

If you have time, Google " Montreal horror stories with condos"

Disadvantages of a condo:
- YOU are not in control of your expenses and have no say. Plenty of times I had clients who had to withdraw $50K from their investments because something happened in their condo. If they did not pay, they would have been forced out.
- Check the story of the condo owners of Boisbriand who were forced to abandon their homes but had to continue to pay their mortgages.
- A lot of people buy a condo, to rent. So imagine if your new neighbor is a pimp and has people coming over at all hours.
- Condos that are turned into Airbnb's, and plenty of damages are done to common areas, and you have to pay a part of that.
- A client once said that someone put a car in their condo, on the top floor. (don't ask me how it was done) The car was a very old car and ended up leaking oil to the condo appartements below, and they were all snowbirds. By the time everyone came back home in April, the damage was so severe, they had to evacuate.
- You are not in control of the condo fees I know someone who has a condo fee of $1200 per month.
- Condo laws might change at any moment, and you will not be allowed pets.

- Condo rules removes your enjoyment of your place. Some condo rules dictate.
  - What color to paint your front door.
  - You cannot do any major repairs or modifications without asking for permission.
  - Trash disposal. (you get fines if you forget to put out your trash bin on the proper day)
  - Usage of holiday decorations
  - Which contractors to use, even if you think they are not qualified.
- When it is time to sell, it might be hard for all of those reasons, especially if the monthly condo fees have skyrocketed.
- There are also plenty of cases of mismanaged funds. You pay monthly condo fees, do you really know what happens to that money?
- Condos do not appreciate as much as a regular detached home.
- Presidents of the condo association who have their own agenda.

If you still want to purchase a condo, I am not sure how to guide you except:

- Make sure you read all the condo association documents, including the minutes of the last 5 years.
- Try to ask a lot of questions, in writing, about the condo association budget, emergency funds and how all that is controlled.
- Since you will NOT have control of expenses of the common areas, make sure you have plenty of savings, or a line of credit.

Chapter Fifteen
Communication about money

In some Facebook groups I have seen posts about women who want to **start a business, and the spouse is not too supportive.** The comments from the other women:

- Leave him, he is not supportive, he does not really love you.
- Stat the business anyway to show him you can do it.

Ok, hold on. I have been on the other side, where the spouse has a new idea every weekend. Or evetime they watch Dragon's Den; it inspires them to invent something.

Some spouses have legitimate fears:

- They have seen you start and drop projects at least 5 times per year.
- You do not do research before starting something, you just dive into crazy ideas like as if there are no financial consequences.
- Instead of using your youngest years to hustle at a real career, you would rather do ANYTHING from home, even if that means making so little money, it does not help the family finances.
- The fear that you will use up all of the family savings, or credit, to start something unprofitable.
- Yesterday you were selling shakes, and today you want to create your own line of makeup.

I have heard it all, and I have shared some stories. Communication with a spouse is important. Building a business plan that respects the family budget is key. Start slowly to build your spouse's trust and appease their fears. One way to protect the family, is to make sure that your company is incorporated, thus protecting the family against any creditors.

Another question that comes back often is about the division of the **family expenses** within a couple.

I will answer simply:
- If you were to use the 50-30-20 rule, then:
  - 50% of your income, and 50% of their income is to pay for common expenses. There should not be too many arguments here, unless one of you was pushing for the expensive cars and house, even though you could not afford it. It also saves future arguments, you do not upgrade your house or your car unless your income increases as well.
  - 30% of your income and their income is for the other things like cell, wifi, trips, outings. Arguments might happen here because one spouse spends too much on shoes, and the other one is collecting expensive guitars. You have to both agree that , within the 30%, if you have money left after the common things like the cell bill, then you can spend it how you like. Each person should have an amount to spend, without the other person freaking out.
  - Then, everything is much easier if you both have 20% to save and invest. **There is nothing worse** than being in a couple, where ALL of your money goes towards the family, and the other person is accumulating retirement money.
  - Discussing this ratio at the beginning of the relationship, and sticking to it, can save your marriage. Math is math, it is easy to base your decisions if you are looking at the math.

The last question I get the most is about **financial literacy,** and this the main reason behind my books.

How young is too young to discuss money, and what do I start with?

- In my book *Wealth 101 for teenagers*, I talk about the *Marshmallow Test* that was done in 1972 by Stanford university. It was a test with pre-k children. (I will let you google it). This showed that some children had restraint and understood that waiting was profitable. Avoiding instant gratification has its rewards. If your children can understand saving money for a future goal, it is the most important thing they can learn.
- As young as 5, you can give them a piggy bank, and teach them how to save. You can give them the option to save, spend, and donate. Saving to buy a bike will discourage them but saving to get $50 to go to the toy store might be a good way to start. I don't really like to give money as a reward for doing a task (because they grow up thinking there should be a reward for doing the dishes, and we all know men who do not help around the house) .
- As young as 8, they can learn about chequing and savings account.
- At 12, they can learn everything from interest, inflation to investments.
- I have conferences with teenagers as young as 12, and believe me, it is not too hard for them to understand.

I want my child to understand about interest, so is there a way to invest for them?

Learning about the magic of compound interest is important, but it is much more important to learn about staying away from instant gratification and saving.

Yes, there is a way for you to save money for them, in a student account at the bank, which probably gives no to little interest.

There is a way to invest money for them, with a Family Trust, or an In Trust account in their name. However, due to the complexity of the accounts, annual reports, and taxation, we normally recommend those accounts to High-Net-Worth individuals who have maximised their TFSA, RRSP and RESP. Reach out if you want to discuss more.

Children listen to your conversations, and especially about money. You might try to teach them about instant gratification but do the opposite yourself. You have to realise that the kids are listening to what you say but are also paying attention to what YOU are doing with your money.

Chapter 16
Understanding your rights in a separation.

You might be less inclined to pay most of the family expenses if you are to find out that if you separate, you get nothing. Plenty of separating individuals think that just because they paid most of the expenses, they are owed half of the house.

Knowing your rights, and obligations, even if you are not even thinking of a separation, will help you make budget decisions.

In most provinces, or states if you are common-law, you get nothing if you separate. Whoever legally owns the house, keeps the house. Whoever legally owns the cars, no matter who drives them, keeps them.

You might have accumulated debt, and the other person accumulated investments, too bad. You might have a legal case, and it is called an "unjust enrichment". An example of this is a woman who stayed with her common-law spouse, and raised their kids, for 25 years. He was building a business while she stayed home for a few years but went back to work. She was paying for most of the bills while the business was not profitable. He waited until the business was worth millions before leaving her. You might not win an "unjust enrichment" claim, so it si much better to know your rights beforehand.

Marriage or civil union contract:

Signing a marriage or civil union contract makes it easier at separation, most of the time, unless you forget to write things in the contract.

I was once talking to a person regarding their divorce situation, and they could not believe how much assets and money they were giving to their ex-spouse. They had signed a marriage contract many years ago, and they thought they could get a lawyer to try to go around what they had signed.

Common-law:

You must understand your rights BEFORE moving in with them and starting a life together. Since every province or state has different rule when it comes to division of assets in a divorce or separation, you have to find out about where you live.

Common-law without kids.
If you are in a common-law relationship, and do not have kids together, you might not have ANY rights at all to any assets, even if you feel like you helped pay for everything. You get to keep what is yours.

Common-law with kids.
The children have rights, and that includes child support and shsared custody. Most states and provinces will give equal rights to both parents. The years where the mother had automatic custody are long gone.

Married

Married couples have the protection of the division of assets, depending on where you live. This might mean that you get 50% of EVERYTHING that grew during the marriage, and that includes :
Real estate
Investments
Air Miles
Insurance policy cash values
Cars
Etc.

It is important to make the distinction between what GREW during the marriage, and what the net worth is at the time of separation. If your spouse was already worth 2 million when you met them, and now they are worth 3 million, you get half of the 1 million, not the 3.

It is also important to note that you do NOT get more assets if the reason behind the separation is because the other person cheated. In Canada, the no-fault divorce was introduced in 1986.

If you are an entrepreneur, it is important to understand that just because it is YOUR business, it does not mean that the other person has no rights to it if you are getting a divorce. If you decide to marry someone, you might want to have a marriage contract that will exclude your current business from the division of assets.

Chapter Seventeen
The sandwich generation

Many women will have the burden of taking care of their aging parents. We are often called the sandwich -generation, because our kids are staying home until they are in their 30's, and at the **SAME time**, you might be taking care of your parents. We are in a financial sandwich, taking care of 3 generations. No other generation before us had this, as children would leave the home earlier than today.

How to prepare and cope?
- Have a discussion with your parents about their wealth, insurance and legal documents, way before it is needed.
- If you have siblings, try to share the physical and financial burden.
- Would your parents rather live with one of you?
  - Live in a bi-generation house?
  - Or in a group home?

Taking care of loved ones could be a huge financial burden. The least expensive option is to have your parents live with you, thus having 3 generations under the same roof. Having a clear budget , and sticking to it , will be very important.

If you are NOT in Canada, everything discussed still applies to you:

- Do you have your legal documents in place?
- Do you have insurance?
- Did you have the money discussion with your spouse?
- Do you know your rights in a case of separation?
- Are you looking to go into real estate as an investment?
- The sandwich generation is very common in other countries as well. How will you cope financially?

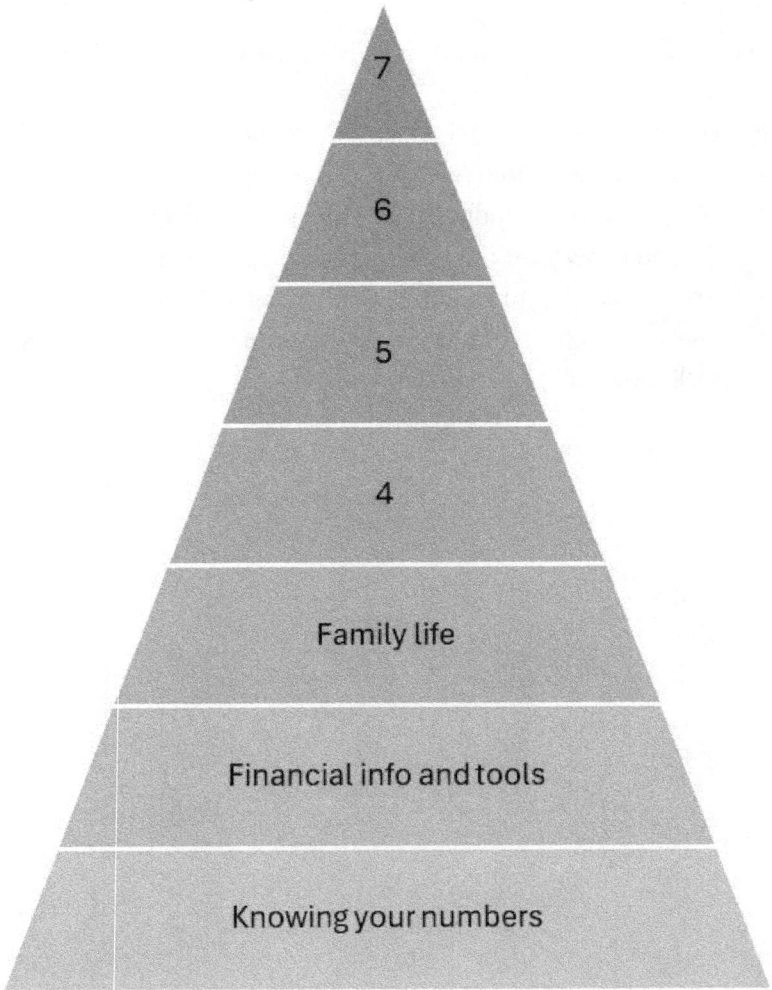

Increasing your income

You can certainly build wealth by cutting your expenses as much as you can and save/ invest the difference.

However, for some, cutting the extra expenses still does not leave any money at the end of the month. For some, those expenses were on credit cards. If your monthly expenses are not all covered by income, the first step is to increase revenues.

There are many ways to increase revenues, from a part-time job to an online business.

We all know that sometimes to have an increase in your salary; you must be willing to work for a competitor. Your experience eventually might be worth a lot more to another firm. Salary is not the only reason to change jobs. Company policies and cultures, benefits, vacation days are some things to look at.

However you want to increase your revenues, you must make sure that you have a plan in place first. Otherwise, when you increase your revenues, you will increase your expenses. (As explained in Oprah's towel theory. The more money we make, the more we spend. Upgrading the car or the house. If your salary increases, do not move, do not upgrade your car.)

One stay-at-home mom I met started working for a MLM company selling make-up. She went from no revenue to a $3000 per month income quickly. She had no advisor, no accountant, no real plan. What happened? Shopping trips, lunches with girlfriends, new cellular phone, expensive new car, whatever, you can imagine.

Come tax-time, she had no savings to pay her income taxes. If she had an advisor in her life, he/she would have told her to save a percentage of that income and would have started a plan for her. Ideally 30%.

If you plan from the start, and be stubborn about it, you will be able to save & invest when your salary increases.

Increasing your income, where to start?

- Are there any positions within your existing firm that would pay you more?
- Is there any competing firm that would pay you more? (we all know that new recruits have at least 5-25% higher salary than someone who has been there for 20 years.)
- Are there positions that would pay you the same for 4 days instead of 5? (this is not a salary increase, but would allow you one day to work on your other projects)
- If your salary is low, are there any courses that you could take to increase your career opportunities?
- Do you have any talents?
- Did you want to develop any talents?
- Are there businesses you would like to have, but do not have the talent for it? Example, a virtual assistant, but you are clueless when it comes to PowerPoint and Excel?
- If your business idea is crazy, and not sure where to start, do you have a group of entrepreneurs that you hang out with, and exchange ideas?
- If you have a business idea, but not sure where to start; the first thing to do is to check in your area to see if there are grants, or government programs.
- Do not go into that MLM because your friend seems to have success in it.
- Do not let yourself get sucked up into a 'business idea' with a friend who is reaching out to you because they figured you have money saved up.

- Are you an expert in your field? if so, there are many ways to make money from that.
    - Writing books
    - Collaborating with other professionals is writing books.
    - Blogs and vlogs (creating or participating in other people's)
    - Podcast (creating or participating)
    - Writing articles for others
    - Look into WeWork, Fiver, or other platforms that hire experts.
- Are you creative?
    - Same thing as above, Fiver and other platforms hire artists for logos and illustrations.
- Do you have a MLM?
    - Are you able to get a downline?
    - Are you able to motivate your downline?
    - Are you able to KEEP your downline?
    - Are you doing things differently than others, that would encourage others to join YOU and not the next MLMer ?
    - (more on the MLM starting on Chapter 18)

Since this is not a 'business ideas' book, I will not go into details of which businesses to start, how to get funding, look for grants, how to hire people and how to manage payroll. That is a completely different book. What I can tell you is that if you decide to start something, keep a budget in place.

A friend of mine, who has savings, wanted to build herself a wellness business. She asked me for advice, these are some tips I gave her:

- Why use your own money to pay to launch your business?
- DO NOT USE YOUR OWN MONEY. (In most cases, it makes sense to keep your savings, use the bank's money. This requires a consultation)
- If you use your own money to launch the business, how will you survive financially if the business does not pick up the first year?
- Banks do not lend money to people who are in trouble financially.
- While your credit score is high, and you have savings, THAT is the time that the bank will give you a loan, not when you have been opened for 2 years, going bankrupt and used up all your savings.
- Make a DETAILED business plan.
- Be stubborn about keeping costs low. For example, if opening a coffee shop, you do NOT have to buy brand new equipment. Starting a business is fun, and getting a bank loan is even better. BUT be smart about every dollar.
- If you do not touch your savings or investments, it means that you are personally building wealth, while your business is starting and growing.
- If your business is Incorporated, the assets and debts are kept separate from personal (unless the bank made you sign a document that you personally guarantee the loan).

- I see it all the time, people who use their retirement money to launch their dream-retirement business. Don't do that. A woman I know spent all her money in a chicken-leg restaurant. ALL her money. It was closed within 6 months. She had to declare bankruptcy and go back to a shitty job. All her retirement money was gone. *Imagine losing all the wealth you have built while you were working in a shitty job, to lose all of it within a few months into entrepreneurship.*
- I also hear all the time stories from family members who get sucked into 'investing' money in a business that a loved one started. "He has been working in that field for 30 years, he knew what he was doing'. Why did he ask family members for money? Probably because the bank did not think it was a good idea.
- Do not give your savings to people who are starting a business. Your own savings should not be touched, for any "once in a lifetime opportunity."
- Do not discuss money with people. Do not tell them that your mortgage is paid off. You have no idea how many people are looking for investors for their next big thing. Most scams start with a "successful' person driving a fancy car. Stay away.

You have to spend money to make money :   I hate that expression.

If you are not in Canada:

 If you are in the USA, there are opportunities to make money. There are some strict business regulations that we have in Canada that do not seem to be as strict in the USA.

For other countries:
write down opportunities that you have that was not listed above. Make sure you understand all costs before getting involved.

Chapter eighteen
Understanding the
MLM

Multi-Level-Marketing.
Some people call it a pyramid.

Someone I know decided to start doing a MLM. She decided that she was going all in.

- She got a "personal coach' that cost $6000 for 4 months.
- She paid a 'marketing expert' whom she paid $800 per month to take care of her social media.
- She paid a virtual assistant to organise things for her
- Bought a new laptop, video equipment, including those fancy ring lights.
- A fancy microphone because she wanted to look professional doing videos on Instagram.
- She joined a very expensive networking group (I am talking thousands per year)
- Her expenses were in the tens of thousands, and she had generated less than $3K of income that year.
- She decided to concentrate on her career , and have this MLM on the side.
- Unfortunately stories like this happen ALL the time!

Deciding to go all in is great. Unfortunately, some people throw money at something, but then do not put the effort. Buying a fancy microphone will not help you get over your fear of public-speaking, if you do not put in the time to build confidence.

Understanding the MLM.

Multi-level marketing is easy to understand. You make money selling products, but you also make money by having people in your downline who are selling the products.

Some people are calling it a pyramid. Pyramid schemes are illegal. A MLM, most of them anyways, are legit. What makes it legal is because you can join today and have the make opportunity to make as much money as the person who started years ago.

Do NOT join because your friend makes it look like fun and easy. One of the main reasons to join is because you love and use the product yourself.

Ask questions before joining like:
- Do you have to keep an inventory?
- What is the cost to join?
- Is there a minimum sale amount per year to keep your status?
- Is there an annual cost to stay an agent?
- Are there other costs, like to have a website?
- How often do you get paid?
- In what currency do you get paid?
- What are the shipping fees?
- What is your 'agent discount" on products?
- Does the platform provide reports, especially reports to use at tax-time?
- What are the rewards?
- Do clients have a fidelity discount?
- Do clients have to purchase a minimum every month?

Chapter nineteen. Building slowly

You can make money with an MLM, and you can make money with any type of home-based business.

My recommendations are:

- Start slowly.
- If you are doing a home-based business, first learn about your city-by laws on home businesses.
- Check to see if you have to tell your home insurance provider and need to get insurance for your clients who come to your house.
- Check with your car insurance, especially if you have inventory in your car.
- Check with your insurance agent if you should get insurance for doing events.
- Check if you need a special license, especially if you think of making food from your house.
- If you are doing a MLM, start with a few products, or a small inventory.
- Penty of people keep their full-time jobs and do this on the side.
- Make sure you understand all expenses , and what will be the monthly budget for this.

- Do not think that family and friends will be your biggest supporters.
- Build yourself a community, and a networking group.
- Do not behave like a vacuum cleaner salesman from the 80's.

The biggest trap in the MLM is that many women spend a LOT of money on inventory, catalos, and other items, and continue to do so, without having the sales for it.

Chapter twenty.

Committing to one.

Ok, we all heard stories of a great chef who opened a restaurant, and it failed within a few months. Not because he was not a great chef, but because he was a chef who had no clue how to run a business. You might think those are the most come type of stories of failed businesses.

What I have seen the most is people who have the shiny object syndrome.

- ✓ Start something,
- ✓ Seeing how much effort it takes.
- ✓ Losing interest.
- ✓ Finding a new shiny object.

What we also often see if someone who is doing multiple things at once, but not being an expert in any of it. Serial entrepreneurship sounds cool, but it is not.

Building one business, and then selling it , to start another, is a great description of yesterday's serial entrepreneur.

I have met a woman who does so many things at once, I lost track. I think these are her current businesses: (example is changed a little, because I do not really know someone who does all of this , but you get my drift)

- ✓ She creates websites.
- ✓ She designs logos.
- ✓ She is a Youtube vlogger, and reads peoples' energy
- ✓ She creates soaps.
- ✓ She sells jewelry , with a MLM company
- ✓ She is a wedding photographer

Believe me, she is NOT an expert with any of that. Her websites are the most basic of websites, her logos look like they were done in the 1980's, her soaps are ok, and her wedding pictures look worse than the pictures we can take with our IPhones. When she is networking, she tells people she does all of that. I would never hire someone who is not constantly working on their crafts. You would not get an electrician, who also dabbles in 5 other completely different fields.

If you do not live in Canada, make a list of ways to increase your income.

Are there any MLM in your country that you want to try?

Are there any home businesses that you could start?

How much money can you afford to spend on that?

How much time do you have per week or per month to dedicate to that?

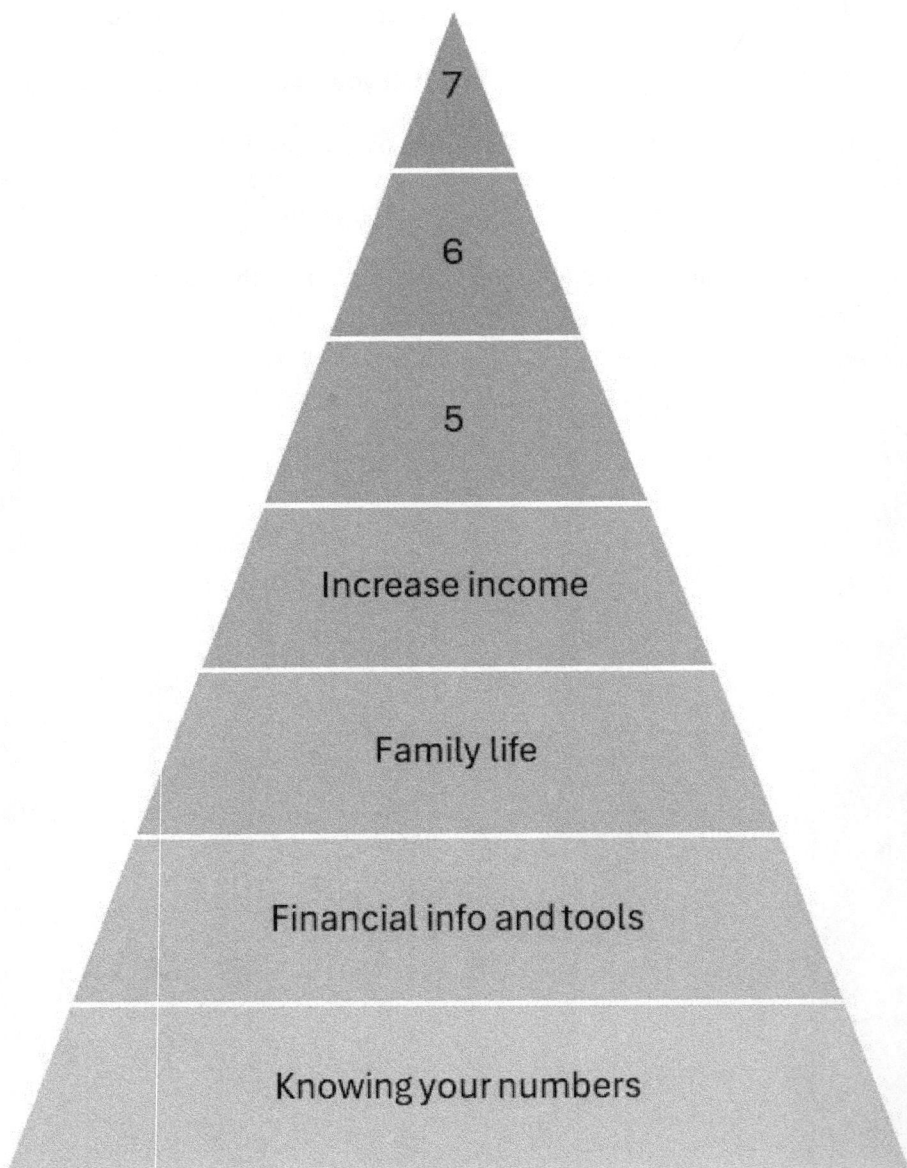

7

6

5

Increase income

Family life

Financial info and tools

Knowing your numbers

Beware of scams

I always tell people this: a stock market crash of 20% is not your biggest worry. Some things to worry about are covered already in this book : you can get sick, you might get the financial burden of other loved ones, your spouse can pass away, your business partner can pass away. One of the ways to lose money quickly is to be a victim of a fraud.

Chapter twenty-one.

Common coaching scams.

I am certainly not talking about coaches, and the money they charge, and if it is effective. I am talking about a coaching scam that I heard about a few years ago.

This is the scam:

- A personal coach approaches you and offers you a program that used to be $50K, and now is only $15K.
- The coach pays attention on how easily you can afford that.
- Once you sign up, and pay, the coach invites you to meet his great financial advisor, who is making huge returns for him.
- The advisor is not licensed at all.

- You transfer your accounts to the new advisor, and eventually lose all of it, and never hear from them again.
- The reason why it works, is because the scammer has 'coaches' who vet how rich the clients are.
- People are more inclined to listen to a third party and are motivated how great their returns are.

The way to protect yourself is:

- Never tell people how much money you have, unless the person is a professional who needs to know.
- Never tell people your salary and that you finished paying off the mortgage.
- Every financial advisor has licenses, and you can check on their regulatory website. (Google it, and ask around)
- Be mindful that sometimes our names might be spelled a little differently on the regulatory body's website, like mine is. Our names are entered as written on our birth certificate.

Chapter twenty-two.

Pump and Dump.

This is something that I have witnessed firsthand, and I was the whistleblower. I was treated like crap for it, but would do it again in a heartbeat.

This is how most Pump & Dumps are done:

- Buy shares of a private company before it comes out as an IPO on the stock market, for example, a million shares at 10 cents.
- Convince an advisor at another firm to do the same.
- Convince the manager of the other firm to do the same and is just so happens that that manager is the father of your associate.
- Convince your associate to also purchase.
- Convince your father and brother to do the same.
- Convince another advisor in your own firm that this will be the stock that will make them millions.
- When it comes out on the market, you buy it for ALL your clients.
- You sell EVERYTHING that they have in their account and you buy that penny stock.

- Every morning, you and the advisors from the other firm discuss how much the price is increasing, and you seem to have insider information.
- You tell your clients to not worry, because news will come out soon, and the price with go way up.
- You tell some clients that if it crashes, you will refund them.
- Once you have purchased for every single client you have and the other advisor have, you try to get more advisors to buy.
- Once you have stopped buying for your clients, the price starts coming down.
- Before you even think to sell, make sure that there is no one who caught on to your scheme, and does not tell on you.
- Sell your million shares for about $1million, the price is now at $1, and you have one million shares. You have a capital gain of $900K, but you do not care.
- Since you sold, the stock starts crumbling, and the clients lose everything.
- PUMP and DUMP.
- You pumped the shares to a price you were excited about, for yourself, and then dumped it.

Of course, this is not what I have witnessed, but you can now guess how it is done.

The way to protect yourself is if your advisor seems way to arrogant with you and tells you to trust them with a penny stock, run. Penny stocks are speculative, and you should not put more than 5% of you investments in it.

Chapter Twenty-Three

Online trading and teaching platforms.

This is probably one of the most popular scams.

Here are the details of the scam:

- You are approached by someone who drives a very fancy car, and they look extremely young.
- They tell you they make **$30-$100K per month** doing FX trading, crypto trading, or regular Stock Market trading.
- They have access to a very cool online platform that teaches you how to do all of that.
- The teaching platform also allows you to do your own trading.
- You can get in this month for as little as $100, but normally it requires $1000, but you must act quickly.
- You are told that depositing money and withdrawing money is as quick as any other banking transaction, 2 days at the most.
- They have been doing it for almost a year and are rich enough to retire.

- They invite you to a zoom, where you meet a lot of millionaires, who say they do this for only a few hours per week.
- You deposit money.
- Your little money grows with high returns that you have never seen before, so you tell others, and you deposit more money.
- It grows so much, that you get excited, and tell more people.
- By the time you want to withdraw your money, it is impossible, and the platform crashes.

I have heard about this type of scam 30 years ago, back then it was mostly about FX trading, and now the hype is with crypto.

Another crypto scam:

The person tells you that they take your Bitcoins, trades them, make you rich, and return them to you for a 2% fee.

You can guess, you will never see those Bitcoins again.

(And that is besides the taxation that comes with gains on crypto. No one would take on taxes for you, and only get 2% return) .

With crypto, do not give your passwords to anyone, but do write it down somewhere in case you were to pass away.

Chapter Twenty-Four

Personal loans

Some private lenders are *legit.* They charge about 12% per year, and if you miss a payment, they go after your house. They are allowed to, you signed a contract that stipulates that.

I am not talking about those private lenders. I am talking about this scam:

- They offer you a loan at 2%.
- They get all your information. You even gave them your banking information because they said they will deposit the money for you.
- They ask for a deposit, let's say it is $2500 to start the process.
- You never hear from them again.
- Sometimes they use your information for identity fraud, but not always, but you are out $2500.

Chapter Twenty-Five

High returns

Of course, I am not talking about that arrogant financial advisor who pretends to always have the highest of returns,

I am talking about this scam:

- You are approached by someone you know who tells you that they have never made this much money.
- The returns are guaranteed, and they receive a monthly amount.
- With that amount, it allows them to go on trips, and go to the restaurant like never before.
- They just ordered a brand-new car and are getting the delivery this month.
- Sounds too good to be true, but you see your friend with a brand-new lifestyle, and want in.
- The person tells you that it is a closed- investment, and there are only a few spots left.
- You give them your investments, you see returns as well, and you tell someone else.
- Then, the advisor and the firm disappear, and you never see your money again. With all the stories, like Madoff, I hope people do not fall for this anymore.

Chapter Twenty-Six.

The real estate scam.

This is the main reason you do NOT tell people that you finished paying off your mortgage. There are two main types of real estate fraud:

Title fraud :

- The person finds out you no longer have a mortgage.
- They steal your identity.
- They go to a bank and apply for a mortgage against your home.
- They steal the title to your home.
- By the time you find out, you might no longer own the home, or there is a mortgage taken out against it.

Foreclosure fraud :

- The person finds out you are having problems making your mortgage payments.
- They trick you into transferring them the title of the property in exchange for a loan .
- They get the title from you, but you never receive the loan/
- They might resell or refinance your home.

To help protect yourself against real estate fraud:

- when applying for a mortgage, deal with licensed or accredited mortgage and real estate professionals
- fully read any documents before signing them
- keep your mortgage information in a safe place
- shred old documents rather than throwing them in the trash
- contact your mortgage lender first if you're having trouble making your mortgage payments
- consult your lawyer or notary before giving another person a right to deal with your home or other assets
- research any company or individual who offers you a loan
- do a land title search with your provincial or territorial land registry office. It will show the name of the property owner and any mortgages or liens registered on the title
- consider buying title insurance to protect yourself against losses from title fraud

Chapter Twenty-Seven
The grandparent scam.

I am sure you have heard of it.

- Someone young calls an elderly person and pretends they are the grandchild.
- They say they are in trouble , but are embarrassed to tell their parent, and they ask you to not tell.
- They say that they must act quick, because they are in jail , and need money now.
- The elderly person rushes to go to the bank.

Another elderly scam :

- They follow the elderly and vulnerable to the bank.
- They listen to the conversation the elderly have with the banker.
- They approach the elderly outside with a sad story, like they are an immigrant with a toothache, and need $2000 for a treatment, but since they are new here, they do not have the medical coverage.
- They force the elderly back into the bank, or to the machine.
- The elderly person thinks they helped someone out with a medical bill

Another common scam :

- Very young kids approach an elderly.
- They say they need a small grocery, because it is their mom' birthday and want to make a cake.
- The elderly agree to pay for a small grocery, but it turns out to be bigger than a cake.
- The kids thank the elderly, but go back to the store and get the money back .

I am sure there are other scams that I could mention here.

I personally know people who were victim of fraud.

It is not always easy to detect.

If in doubt, reach out to someone in the financial field that you trust.

Have a discussion with your parents about all the frauds going on, including the call that says you will go to jail because you owe money to the government.

If you do not live in Canada, you have probably heard about the different types of scams in your country. The government often has a section on their websites that alerts their citizens on the current scams .

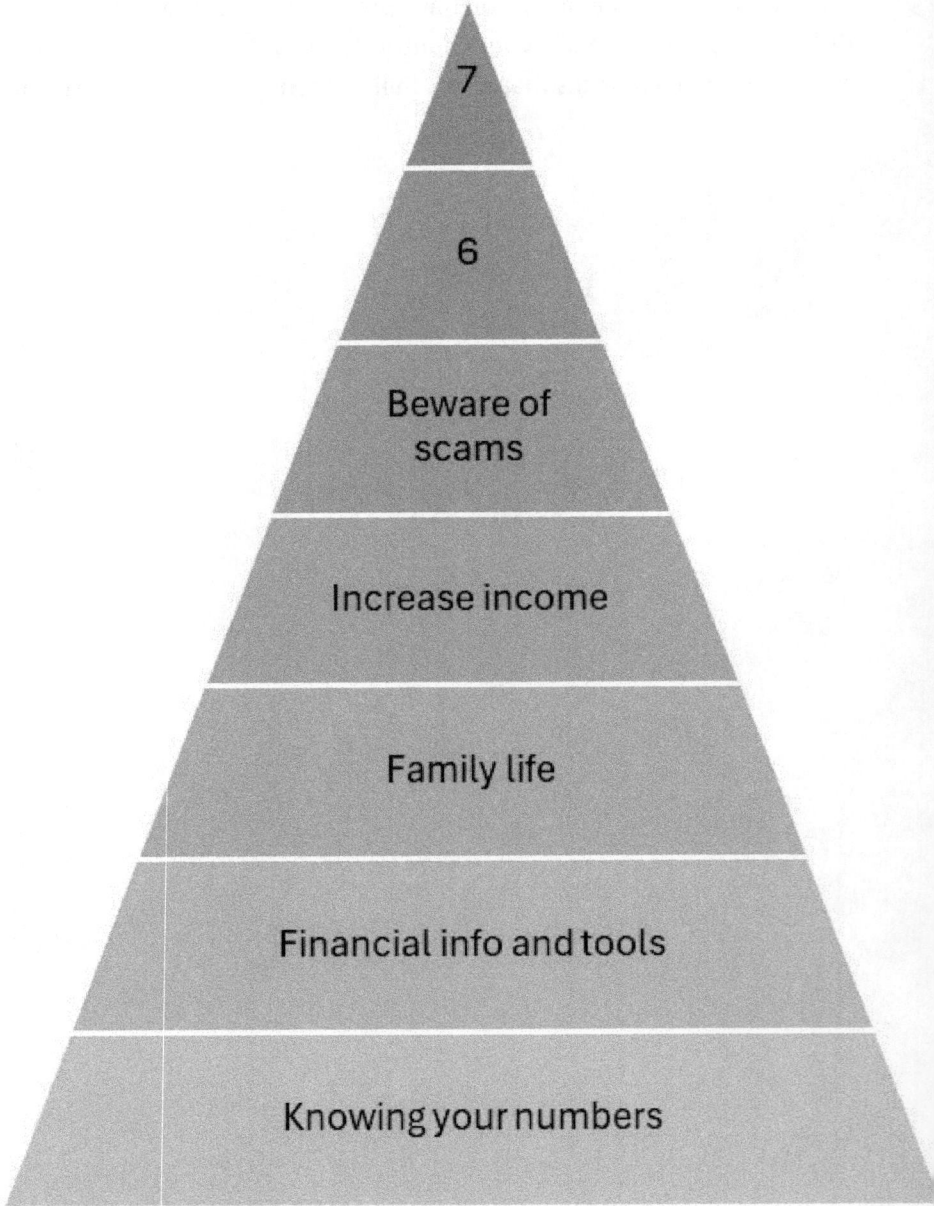

7

6

Beware of
scams

Increase income

Family life

Financial info and tools

Knowing your numbers

The power of the feminine energy and creativity

Chapter Twenty-Eight

The power of the feminine energy and creativity.

If you know me personally, you know that I believe in energy, mediums, astrology and all of that. You can have an analytical mind and have a creative side. You can believe in science and believe in spirituality.

The reason it has a place in a book about Wealth 101 for women entrepreneurs, is because women who succeed in business and build tremendous wealth, often have understood how both the masculine and feminine energy have a role in business.

The masculine energy is about:

- Getting things done
- Achieving quotas.
- Modeled by logic and reason.
- Gathering assets.
- Beating the competition.

The feminine energy is:

- Intuitive
- Oriented towards receiving and nurturing.
- They are in the moment.
- They are balanced.
- They live in harmony.
- Have a greater sense of fulfillment.
- Enjoy being part of a community.
- Can build relationships easily.
- Powerful
- Senses the invisible.
- Loving and creative

To build a business, a career, and especially wealth, women have to be in tune with both of the masculine and feminine energy.

I have seen women so much in the masculine energy that they push away every female friendship. It is hard to build a successful MLM, If you cannot build loving relationships.

I have also seen women so much in their feminine energy that they are not achieving any of the financial goals they have set out.

Understanding that you need both energies to bring you the financial success that you deserve, is the key. With your masculine, you can negotiate a higher salary and be driven to achieve specific financial goals.

With your feminine, you will build relationships that will nourish your business , and you will have creative ideas that will differentiate your business from others.

I have spoken to a friend of mine many times about the feminine and wanted to get a quote from her.

I asked her the following question :

How does the feminine energy help with building wealth ?

When you choose to honour yourself, live your best life and honour your feminine intuition, that's when the flow of abundance really starts to pour in .

Sonya Sun Heart.

Owner of Studio Regeneration.

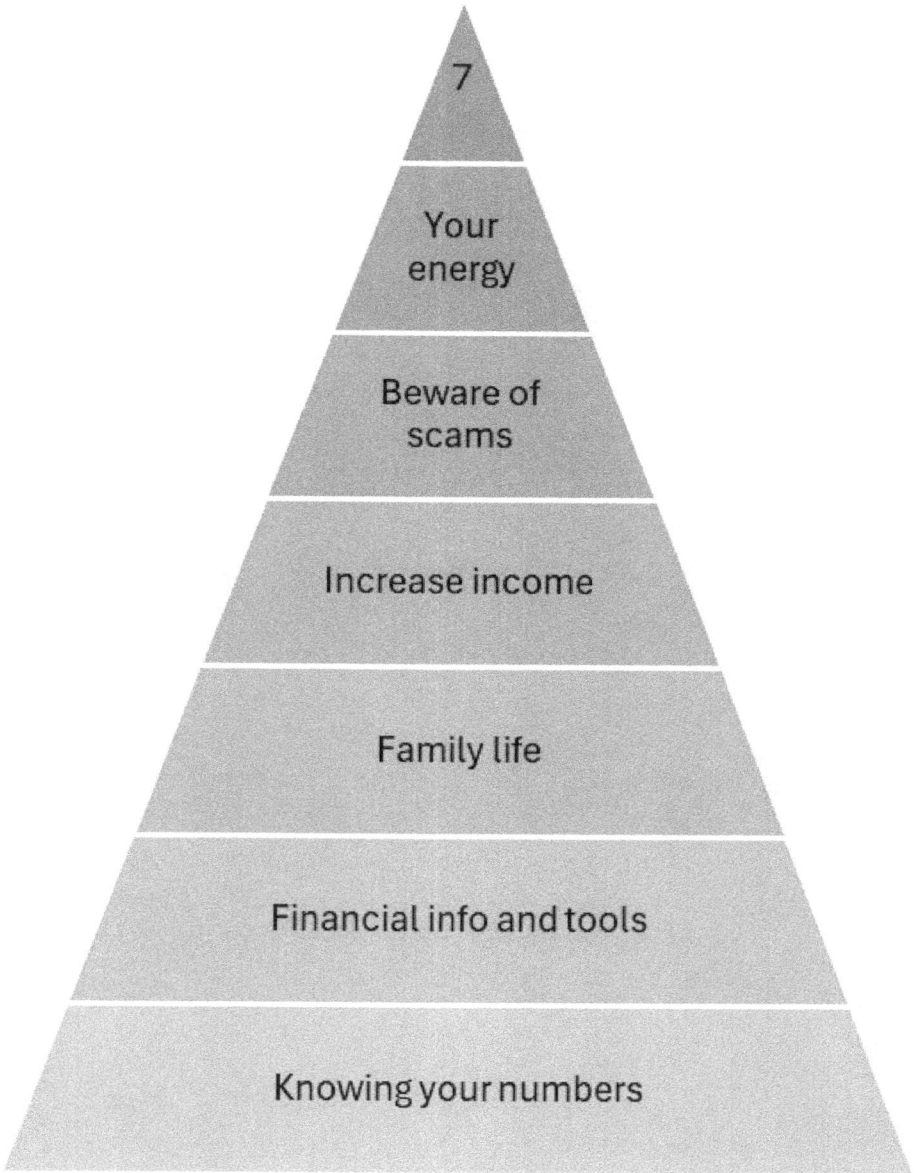

7

Your energy

Beware of scams

Increase income

Family life

Financial info and tools

Knowing your numbers

How to build wealth yourself

Chapter Twenty-Nine

Asset Allocation

We often meet people who want to do things themselves, including doing their own investments. It is not something I recommend, and if I was busy in another career, I would not do it myself. You might KNOW how to do it, but do you really want to spend time taking care of it all ?

If your answer is yes, and you have read this whole book, and still want to do all of that by yourself, there is something you MUST really understand, and that is Asset Allocation.

Asset Allocation is:

- a way of investing your three main categories of assets :
    - Stocks
    - Fixed income
    - Cash
- Real Estate, crypto, or even Art , fall outside these main categories. Some call these speculative, or alternative assets.
- We normally decide what percentages the 3 will be, based on a few factors :
    - Your main goal
    - Your risk tolerance
    - Time horizon
- You can guess that if someone's goal is to make a good return, will be invested differently than someone who's only goal is to NOT lose money.
- You can also guess that someone who has a short horizon, for example, their retirement is in 5 years, they will be invested differently than for someone who is retiring in 30 years.
- Once you know the goal, risk tolerance and horizon, you can come up with an asset allocation that suits those:
    - An Asset Allocation with 20 % cash, 60% fixed income and 20% stocks : you can guess is a conservative portfolio.
    - An Asset Allocation with 5% cash, 15% fixed income, and 80% stock is a growth portfolio.
    - As asset Allocation with 50% Stocks and 50% Fixed Income is a balanced portfolio.

- Market timing and day trading are NOT what will bring success to your portfolio. Over 96% of the success will be because of asset allocation.
- If you want to do your own trades, and think you will go 100% conservative, because you are afraid of the market, then , you missed the point, and should not even invest in the stock market.
- A conservative portfolio will bring you an average of 2% returns.
- A balanced portfolio will bring you an average of 4-6% returns.
- A growth portfolio about 8-12% returns.
- These returns are never guaranteed.

What we also often see if people buying a stock, based on a tip from a friend. Will the friend tell you when it is time to sell ? We have tools, alarms, and analysts that are there to tell us when to sell, who will tell you ?

You can keep doing your own trading if you consistently have good returns. Keep in mind that only 15% of the wealthy individuals have built their wealth without the use of an advisor.

Chapter 30
The magic #4

You have built wealth and are about to retire. How much do you withdraw without liquidating your portfolio before death ? If the goal is to have money until you pass away, the magic number is 4%.

If you want to leave money to your beneficiaries after you pass away, then you should withdraw 2 or 3% or your money, or investments per year.

Well, it used to be 4%, when I was studying all my courses. This is when inflation was kept at about 2%. I think you will understand where the 4% comes from :

Let's say you have a portfolio that has an objective of growth.

- Makes a steady return of 8%
- Inflation is 2%
- You withdraw 4%
- That leaves 2% in the portfolio to help continue to grow.

When it is time to withdraw money from your portfolio :

We can ask you how much you NEED to survive.

Or if you have built enough wealth, we can tell YOU how much money you can withdraw per year. (again ,the magic number used to be 4%)

It is a calculation.

Our calculations are harder to do when inflation is not steady.

If you made a financial plan while inflation was crazy high, redo your plan once the inflation drops .

Another example :

- You have a balanced portfolio that makes a steady return of 5%
- Inflation is 2%
- We will tell you to withdraw only 1%
- To leave 2% in the portfolio to allow it to grow.
- If you tell us that 1% is not enough : we can either increase the risk of your portfolio, or you will probably will not have enough money in the portfolio until you pass away.

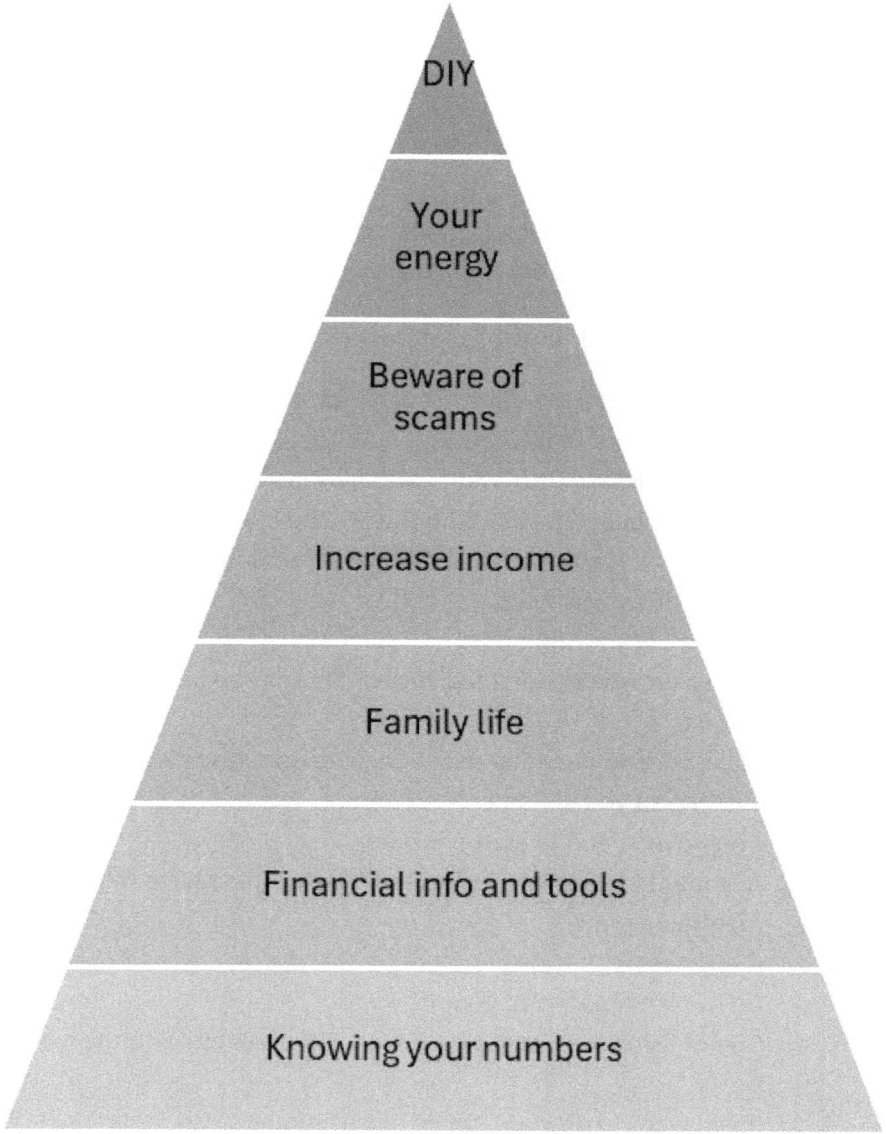

DIY

Your energy

Beware of scams

Increase income

Family life

Financial info and tools

Knowing your numbers

Summary :

If you want to build wealth, and ignore the other things in this book, your biggest risk is not a stock market crash.

If you want to build AND protect your wealth along the way , you will :

- o Get a Will and a Mandate for you and spouse
- o Get life, CI and DI insurance.
- o Have those hard discussions with parents and siblings.
- o Follow a budget, ideally with the 50-30-30 rule. The more money you make, the ratio still stays the same, it will be the $$ amount that will go up.
- o Know all of your numbers
- o Make sure you understand your rights in a separation and divorce.
- o Make sure you understand your coverages at work and get coverage if you are an entrepreneur.
- o Don't overspend to start a business.
- o Anyone that goes into business with you, must have their *shit* together as well.
- o A business with a partner needs a shareholder agreement.
- o Do not lend money to people.
- o Do not listen to people who have a 'business opportunity for you"
- o If you want to do your own investing, understand Asset Allocation.

If you are an entrepreneur:

- o putting tings in place to protect yourself is even more important than someone who has the safety net of an employer and a group plan.
- o If your budget is limited, start with one thing, and build from there. One thing to look into is the Disability Insurance (some people call it a salary insurance).
- o Since you are not building a pension with work, make sure you are saving enough.

END